MY PENCIL MADE ME DO IT

A Guide to Sketchnoting

CARRIE BAUGHCUM

EduGladiators
NEW ERA OF LEADERSHIP ENGAGEMENT & ADVOCACY.

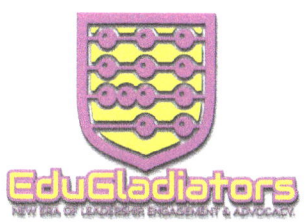

Published by EduGladiators LLC
www.edugladiators.com

Copyright © 2019 by Carrie Baughcum

All rights reserved. This book, or parts thereof, may not be reproduced in any form without permission.

Paperback ISBN: 978-1-7336864-6-4
E-book ISBN: 978-1-7336864-7-1
LCCN: 2019909523

Book Design & Production: Columbus Publishing Lab
www.ColumbusPublishingLab.com

Printed in the United States of America
1 3 5 7 9 10 8 6 4 2

Praise for *My Pencil Made Me Do It*

"I'm one of Carrie's toughest customers of the 'I can't draw' mentality, and she has seen my excitement first-hand when I realized there are some things I CAN draw. That excitement led me to dabble, yet using the idea of 'sketchnoting' in my curriculum was still too daunting.

"This book swept me up in the passion that my students will feel as I use Carrie's ideas about visual learning in the classroom each and every day. *My Pencil Made Me Do It* convinced me there is no one way—and no wrong way—to start using the power of student-created visuals in the classroom."

—Joy Kirr, author of *Shift This*, 7th grade ELA teacher

"This book is stacked with practical strategies and colorful stories to help you and your students get started drawing thoughts and thinking visually. Easy-to-use techniques are detailed through fun and engaging exercises. Beyond helping you learn the art of sketchnoting, this book takes you on an emotional journey of self-confidence and growth. I felt empowered to draw and inspired to encourage others to sketch their own thoughts too! This book made me realize that visual thinking and drawing those visualizations are powerful tools that can be used by just about anyone to improve learning! But don't take my word for it! Read it for yourself and learn how to draw your own conclusions!"

—Christopher Bugaj, author of *The New Assistive Tech: Make Learning Awesome For All*, Inclusive Design Facilitator

"There's more than a touch of Carrie's magic in this book; be prepared for your brain, heart, and hands to transcend labels, levels, and preconceived notions of ability. Her deep love and passion for what she does are more than evident, and this energetic read highlights her knack for bringing out the best in others, with others. At its core, sketchnoting/visual note-taking is about connecting with humans, and the way she shows this demonstrates her immense gifts as an educator. Your journey together will explore the magic of questioning, the power of imagination, and of course, a how-to to create your own legendary learning mascot! (Because you simply cannot have this much fun without sharing!) Suffused with Carrie's energy and enthusiasm, everything about this book shouts interaction and engagement with ideas, content, and your learners. It will indeed bring out the very best in who you teach and what you create. Bet you can't read it without smiling. Boom pow."

—Wendi Pillars, Author of *Visual Note-taking for Educators: A Teacher's Guide to Student Creativity*, EAL Teacher

"Read. This. Book. In its pages you will find a friend. It will inform you of all things sketchnoting...the brain research, the theories, the stats, but most importantly, it will CARRIE you through the fun and creativity that oozes from its very soul. Carrie invites you to be a visual thinker, a doodler, and an instant friend."

—Dana Ladenburger, Instructional Coach
Technology Integration Specialist

"It doesn't matter if you are a novice or have Picasso-level talent. Carrie has created the perfect guide to energize your own thinking around sketchnoting as well as teach your students how to do the same!"

—Marlena Gross-Taylor, Social Commerce Entrepreneur,
EduGladiators Founder, Author, Speaker

CONTENTS

Foreword by Matt Miller   7

Introduction   13

PART I: 15

PART II: 23

PART III: 51

PART IIII: 68

PART V: 83

PART VI: 110

About the Author   115

Foreword by Matt Miller

My first sketchnote was a hot mess. It wasn't even a sketchnote, per se. On a cold winter day in Indiana, I was at home with my school-issued iPad. As I often did, I sat on the couch and scrolled through Twitter, looking for something fun to inspire me and my teaching.

I stopped on a tweet by Amy Burvall (@amyburvall) that she had drawn on her iPad. In Carrie Baughcum's words, I thought, *Holy wow! These are so cool!* I downloaded the Paper app she used and got started.

As I mentioned earlier, hot mess. My handwriting was just as messy digitally as it was on paper. My drawings could have been mistaken for a fifth grader's. (You'll learn in this book that that's not the kiss of death!) But it was so much fun! I kept going, leaning into my growth mindset. "You're not an expert at this…yet."

I'm still no expert. But I've seen the power that sketchnotes have over the brain. They stir up the best of our thinking, our creativity, and our personality into a delicious soup that we can serve to others. They lock ideas and learning away in our brains like a vault. And they can make learning joyful!

Speaking of joyful, you're going to LOVE what Carrie Baughcum has created for you in this book. Here's why:

- Her vocabulary—barfy, holy wow, oh my gawsh—is uniquely Carrie.
- You'll fall in love with her fun-loving personality from the first chapter.
- She is fun-loving, but she has a jagged, raw honesty. If she struggled, failed, or even heard voices of doubt, she'll tell you.
- Carrie empowered her students to learn with sketchnotes. She shares that journey generously.
- There's science in sketchnoting. Through dual coding theory and metacognition, she'll show you why visual thinking is serious learning.
- This book is a toolbox with questions and graphic organizers you can start using immediately.
- It's based on a process you can really use: discover, learn, visualize, connect, doodle, repeat.
- Carrie walks the walk and shares her own sketches, bringing ideas to life.

Dig deep, down to the roots with the ideas in this book. If you practice them yourself, you'll unlock this innate creativity and thinking you never knew you had—or you knew it was there but you couldn't reach it. If you bring these ideas into the classroom, you'll see your students thrive in ways you might not expect.

Oh, and there will be smiles. From you. From your students. If you don't get anything else, the smiles will be worth your time and effort.

Matt Miller
Author of *Ditch That Textbook,*
and an always-improving novice sketchnoter

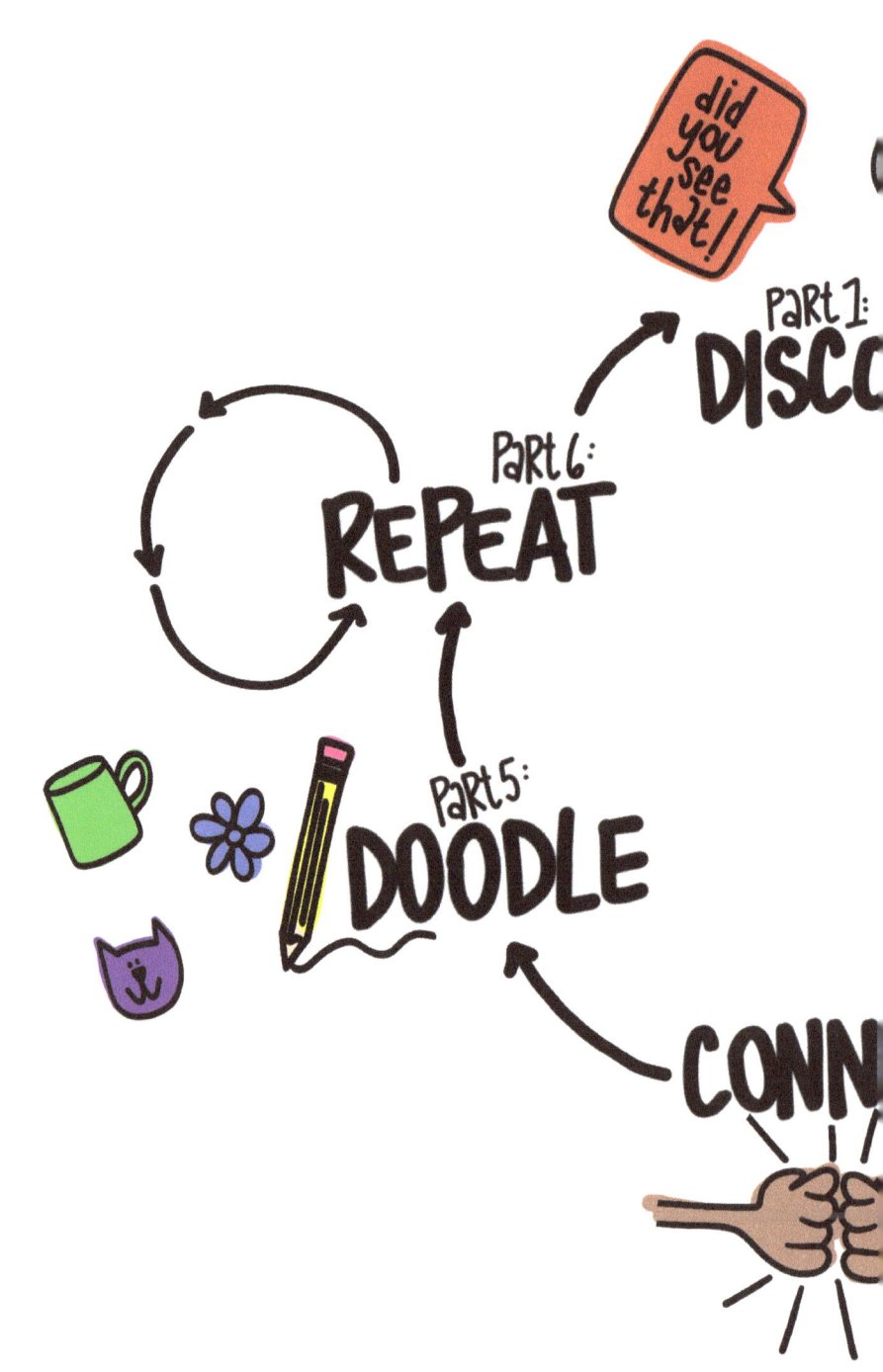

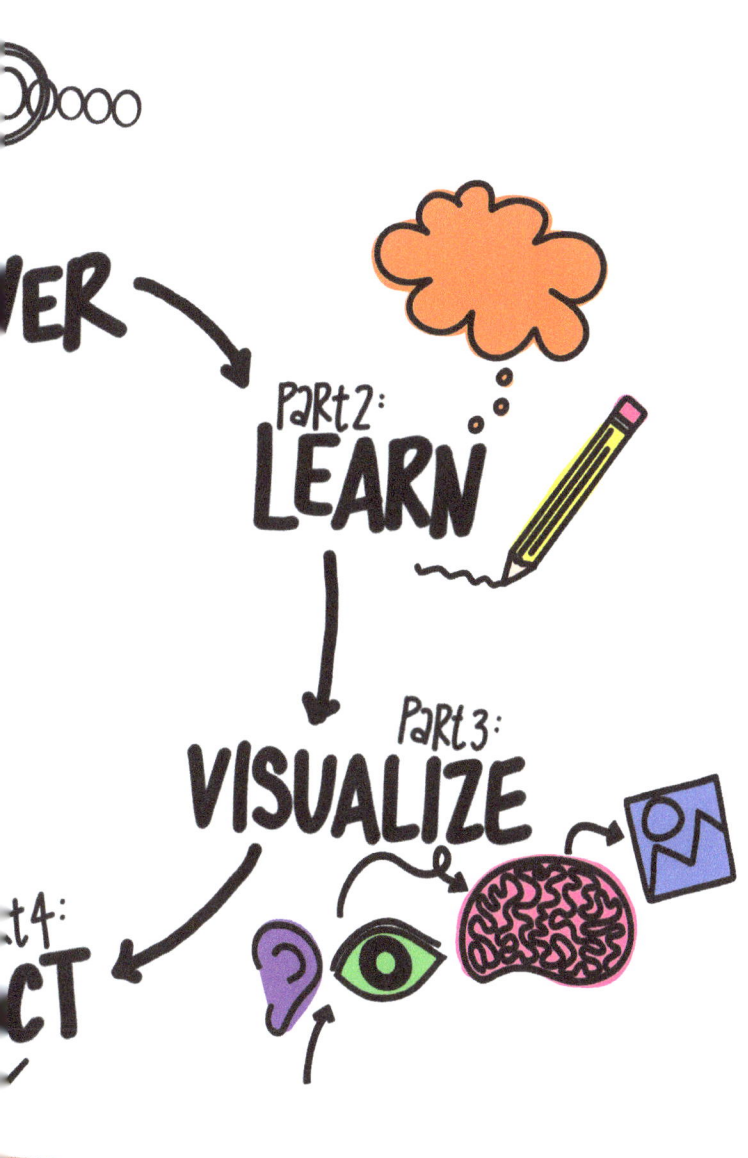

This book is dedicated to you. It is dedicated to the connections we've made, the lessons you've taught me, the talks we've had, the work we've done, the classroom you've been part of and the love you have given me. You will forever be are a part of my journey, part of me, who I am and who I will become.

Introduction

It all started with a conversation with a friend in my kitchen, my iPhone in video mode and the scary dream, tugging passion, barfy leap in fear, creative pull to vlog (video blog...like on camera, for everyone to see, like my actual face), and the deep passion that bringing out the best in ourselves, our students, our children isn't about doing it this way or that way. And it isn't about following these rules to success, using these tools, only using this tech, those strategies, these specific methods or ideas only the way they are intended to be used. It is about connecting with humans. It is about seeing what things, ideas, and tools can do, what strategies can do—stretching them to see what they are capable of. It is about connecting their strengths to our strengths and optimizing the heck out of each of them. It is about looking deep into our hearts and asking ourselves, *Does this help me, does it help them, does it work for me, will it work for them, does this make me happy, does this way work for me?* And when we answer heck yes, connecting that tool, that resource, that strategy, that feeling it gives us to the awesome in each of us. The awesome within each of our students, our children, and within ourselves. It is about connecting weaknesses and using the tools, the tech, the strategies, the methodology and the idea to bring out the very best in each of us.

So find a comfy chair, grab your favorite beverage, and forget everything you think you know about the way we have to learn. Forget how we have to create. Let go of how we think we have to teach. Then make a choice to have the most fun connecting with, soaking up, diving into and learning how to use what visual thinking and doodling to learn can do to bring out the best in you, your students, in learning, in creating or just being you. And if, on this journey, fear starts to whisper, others start to look at your paper and wonder, or you start to feel a flutter of happiness in your heart….tell them that your pencil made you do it!

Part 1: DISCOVER

My children have never known a moment in their lives that they haven't loved to draw. For them, connecting images to words, telling stories with their own combination of doodles and stories, came as natural as breathing. Funny thing is, it wasn't the same for me. Until I became a mother, I couldn't remember the last time I drew, let alone the last time I loved drawing. I especially couldn't remember the last time I could put pencil to paper, fill in the blank space, and not worry

about someone looking at what I had drawn and be terrified I'd be judged on my "artistic" ability, be compared to others, or be told my drawings sucked.

Then it happened. Night after night, my children would grab their favorite crayons and a stack of scratch paper, sit at the dinner table, and doodle and write and giggle while I cooked dinner. Night after night, this would go on. In between stirs and dashes of seasoning, I would walk over to them and ask them about what they were drawing. They would smile, giggle, and light up as they'd tell me elaborate tales about the misspelled words and wiggly stick figures they had drawn.

It didn't take long before spending time with my children meant me picking up a crayon and drawing with them. Drawing with them became our love language. Our time spent at the kitchen table or lying on our bellies on the living room floor, smiling, laughing, sharing space and time creating stories of our world. This time together drawing created wonderful and special moments for us. Weeks and then months went by. They were filled with us writing stories and drawing together. Weeks and months went by and I simply could not shake the happiness that drawing with them brought me. I could not shake the smile I had any time I drew a funny saying that one of them had said that day, combined with my own doodles. I couldn't shake the pride I felt to show them what I had created. I couldn't shake this new feeling…look at me! I can draw…me! I can draw. Me, a mom, me, a teacher, me…I CAN DRAW. I am drawing and I LOVE IT!

For two years, I spent evenings and weekends sprawled out on the floor. I gigged and doodled with my children. All of our words and doodles were safe with each other. It didn't matter how we spelled words, how many fingers our stick figures had, how oversized their heads were, or how weird the wiggly the legs we drew turned out. We shared with each other, valued each other's creations, cherished this time together, and so, so, so loved each other's imaginations, each other's creativity, each other's stories, and each other's doodles.

Each new doodle completed a story. Each story I shared was a chance for me to share my wit, my sense of humor, and my personality! It was so much fun! Yet, no matter how many times my inner doodler spoke to me, nudged me, or reminded me of how happy drawing made me…no matter how much I loved it or how much it filled me up, I could not bring myself to share my doodles and stories with others.

Then it happened.

It was one Christmas Eve after a trip to the mall. Seriously, who shops on Christmas Eve? Well, I did. Yep, you guessed it. It was a madhouse. It was also an experience filled with moments of "are you kidding me" and "no way," and a song made up by my daughter and me about how people drive in the mall parking lot on Christmas Eve. Each of these silly, crazy, pull-your-hair-out, laugh-about-it-later moments became a blog post. Only this time, I didn't write my usual blog post. This time, I wouldn't add a photo from Instagram to my words. This time, I would handwrite and doodle my story. I would doodle, swirl, and color this crazy adventure, intertwining it with the words of my story.

This time, I would share my doodles. I would share my handwritten words for everyone to see on my blog. Gulp. I took deep breaths. I tried not to barf, and I waited in fear to be judged. I waited to be told, "Who do you think you are to share this?"

"What, do you think you are an artist or something?"

"This is an awesome sketchnote," the Facebook comment said.

What the heck is a sketchnote? I thought.

A few Google searches later, and I learned about this thing, this idea of combining words and drawings together. Days passed and life went on. I just could not shake that word, sketchnote. It was actually a thing and people did it on purpose.

All of that time I had spent doodling, writing, and storytelling with my children, not only did it have a name, but it also was an actual thing. It had an impact on companies, collaboration, people, and learning. Sketchnoting, or visual note-taking, was a process and a powerful one at that. There were articles about it, books, too!

Kevin Thorn (Nuggethead.net) defined it as: "A form of Visual Writing by expressing ideas, concepts, and important thoughts in a meaningful flow by listening, processing, and transferring what you hear by sketching either by analog or digital."[1]

Mike Rohde, author of *The Sketchnote Handbook: The Illustrated Guide to Visual Note Taking*, said, "Sketchnotes are rich visual notes created from a mix of handwriting, drawings, hand-drawn typography, shapes and visual elements like arrows, boxes and lines."[2]

---

1   Thorn, Kevin, Nuggethead Studioz. September 03, 2013. https://nuggethead.net/2013/09/sketchnote-school-6-steps-to-great-conference-sketchnotes.

2   Rohde, Mike. *The Sketchnote Handbook: The Illustrated Guide to Visual Note Taking*. San Francisco Calif.: Peachpit Press, 2013.

Doug Neil of Verbal to Visual stated, "Sketchnoting is a form of note-taking, hence the 'noting' part of it, but as you might guess it involves bringing more visuals into the process compared to typical note-taking, hence the 'sketch' part." He added, "The whole idea behind adding sketches to your notes is that it taps into parts of your brain that would lie dormant if you only use words to explore ideas. It's the combination of the two that's most powerful–using both words and visuals while taking notes."[3]

Holy wow, this was really a thing and um, there was science behind this process. All this backed up to this drawing and creating things I loved. Who'd have guessed it?

Months passed and I kept drawing.

I drew by myself.

I drew on the weekends.

I drew with my children.

I drew after dinner.

I fell in love with drawing.

I could not shake the feeling… Drawing made me happy!

It made me happier than I ever remembered feeling about creating something, something that was all mine from my very own imagination and my own mind. I loved every second of it. I loved being able to experience life and to be able to take the craziness, the insanity of motherhood, the moments from my classroom, and the snapshots of life. To be able to write about them, close my eyes, connect the words with the pictures in my imagination, and draw them.

Still, each time I drew and shared my "sketchnote" on social media, I had to take a deep breath, try not to barf, and battle the voices that whis-

---

3   "What Is Sketchnoting?" Verbal To Visual. July 04, 2019. https://www.verbaltovisual.com/what-is-sketchnoting/.

pered to me, *Your ideas are crap, who do you think you are to think you can draw, and who told you that you could draw?*

Then I wrote and drew some more.

Winter came and it was time for my state's annual educators conference. This idea of sketchnoting/visual note-taking was something I wanted to try more. I wanted to try it when listening to people speak. I wanted to take notes on the important parts of what they said, connect with them, and draw what I imagined when I heard their words. I couldn't fight the urge. I had to try it. I wanted to try it in real life, like with other people around, like in public. Double gulp. So I went to the local hobby store and bought a sketchbook, some new pencils, a fine-tip permanent marker, and a package of Sharpie markers. Then I went home, did some more research about sketchnoting and how the "pros" did it in public. The "real sketchnoters," the purest, only draw in pen. No pencil! Just get out there and draw, the "pros" said. Make sure to prep your sketchnote first. Pre-write the title, pre-pick your colors: one main color, a supporting color, and a shadow color; understand your structures and know your topic, the "pros" said. With my sketchbook in hand and a pencil case I borrowed from my child, jam-packed full of all my Sharpies, a pencil, a pencil sharpener, and an eraser, I was ready to "sketchnote" live.

I found a seat in the front next to my friends, opened my sketchbook, and pulled out my pencil case and my eraser. I was ready.

"But real sketchnoters don't sketchnote in pencil, Carrie," the voice whispered.

The keynote started.

Her words filled me up as I focused on every idea she shared. I soaked up her words and waited for the right ones to connect with my heart. I wrote them. Each new phrase and idea that was meaningful to me became part of the paper. I imagined those words and my mind was filled with an image. I drew it next to the words and I smiled at myself. I was sketchnoting. As the keynote went on, I could not take my mind or eyes off of her words and ideas. It was like she was filling me up and I was connected with her. I had never been more focused, listened more intentionally, and had never been happier while learning.

"But you didn't know how to draw all the drawings, Carrie," the voice whispered.

"You used pencil. Real sketchnoters don't use pencil," it nagged.

"You had to use Google images to see how to draw something. A real sketchnoter just knows how to draw them," it berated.

"Look, the keynote is done and your sketchnote still needs to be colored. A real sketchnoter would have had it all done. Real sketchnoters would have done it perfectly." It crushed me.

Wrapped up in that February conference day was all the research that backs why visual thinking and connecting doodles to learning is so powerful. A moment filled with all the reasons why it is so very powerful. Sketchnoting/visual note-taking has the incredible ability to do amazing things with our brains and our hearts.

Metacognition

In "Better Learning through Better Thinking,"[1] Shawn Taylor defines metacognition as an appreciation of what one already knows, together with a correct apprehension of the learning task and what knowledge and skills it requires, combined with the ability to make correct inferences about how to apply one's strategic knowledge to a particular situation and to do so efficiently and reliably. Super-simply put, metacognition is "thinking about

---

1 Shawn Taylor (1999) Better Learning through Better Thinking: Developing Students' Metacognitive Abilities, Journal of College Reading and Learning.

your thinking." It makes learners' thinking active, a strategic activity that strengthens connections. Metacognition challenges us to slow down, think about how and what we are thinking, and forces us to connect it to our learning. It pushes us to be self-reflective, self-assess, iterate, change, grow, and move forward.

Dual Coding Theory

Dual coding is the combination of words and images that facilitates and enhances learning. It is based on the *dual coding theory* (Paivio, 1971),[2] which uses the idea that humans need either verbal associations or visual imagery to increase learning effectiveness. The theory is built on the idea that we have two separate but connected sides of our brain. One side represents and processes nonverbal objects/events (i.e. imagers), and the other side deals with language (words and text). Basically, we have two halves of our brain, one thinking in words and the other thinking in pictures. When they work together, the connections and our learning are stronger and more solidified.

Thinking Visually

Thinking visually is thinking and learning in pictures. Our mind takes in information that we see, read, and/or hear, connects it to what we already know, and formulates an image of what we are learning. In sketchnoting, language icons are simple visual representations, images, objects, elements,

---
[2] Last Updated November 30th, 2018 07:01 Pm. "Dual Coding Theory (Allan Paivio)." InstructionalDesign.org. https://www.instructionaldesign.org/theories/dual-coding/.

and/or ideas. They are the doodle of the image we imagine when we think. This image we imagine connects what we know with what we are learning.

All Learners

Humans have a variety of learning, strengths, and weaknesses. Learners take in information and connect with it in a variety of different ways. The sketchnoting/visual note-taking process taps into the variety of ways our brain processes information, learns, and connects. This allows learners to not only make the process their own, but it also enhances our learning strengths while compensating for our learning weaknesses.

Biological

From the time we are born, our brains love visuals. Visuals and images are the first ways we communicate, tell stories, and share our experiences. Most of all, our brains LOVE visuals! Not only can our eyes process images faster than text, but images are also language-less and enhance our memory and recall of information.

Emotional Connections

Our body loves visuals too. More specifically, it loves drawing them. The act of drawing, doodling, and/or coloring is an act of self-regulation. It centers us, calming us when we are upset and bringing back our focus when our energy is low. Drawing and doodling are also fun and they make us happy.

My Pencil Made Me Do It

MY PENCIL WAS WRITE… That night, I went back to my hotel room and I pulled out my favorite colored Sharpies. I chose the colors of my childhood, bold, colorful, and wide ranging. I began by outlining the words and images in black permanent marker. Then I colored the images, added accent colors, drew underlines, highlighted important words, and signed my name to it.

"You used pencil. Real sketchnoters don't use pencil," the voice lied.

"Your sketchnote still needed to be colored in later, after the keynote. A real sketchnoter would have gotten it all done at the keynote," it lied again.

"Look at all those colors you used. Where are the shadows and accent lines? A real 'sketchnoter' only needs three colors," it lied some more.

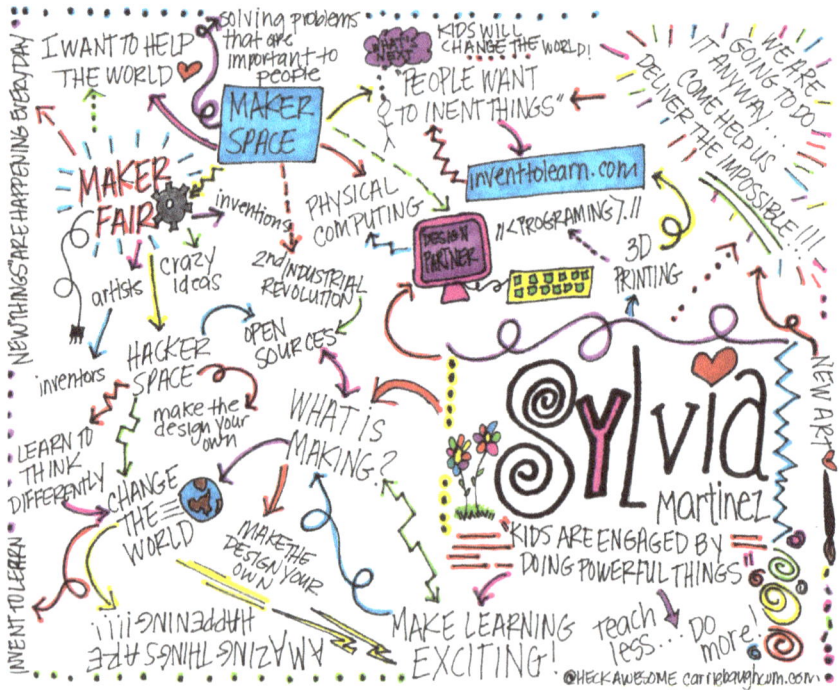

"Ha! You put your name on this. What, do you think you're an artist or something? Who do you think you are?" It lied one more time.

I took out my phone. My hands shook. Then I smiled. I laughed. I took a deep breath and I snapped a picture of MY SKETCHNOTE and shared it on Twitter *#ILoveToDraw*.

Wrapped in that February day was more than just an experience that proved all the science. Something else happened. That day, a new breed of sketchnoter was created. A visual thinker, a learner who doodles, and someone who now believes so deeply in the power of visual thinking and doodling to learn process.

Someone who learned…

Sketchnoting's power wasn't in finishing it at the end of the keynote, capturing all the ideas shared, writing in pen, or drawing the perfect image to connect the learning. Its magic, its power, its real muscle was in the process. Because when we embrace the process, when we trust what feels right to us, when we listen to what works for us, when we fight through the it-has-to-be-done-this-way, it-has-to-be-perfect, this-is-the-right-way, and we hold on, hug, and grab on tight to *how it works for me*…amazing things happen.

This experience and new learning filled me up. I just could not get enough of all of it. I had to dive deeper and learn more.

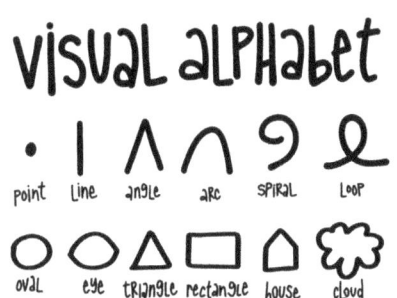

This time, I wanted to learn about visualizing and doodling to learn how-tos and parts that made up sketchnotes. First, I learned about something called a "Visual Alphabet"—a "set of symbols that could easily be learned (like a b c d e f g, 0 1 2 3 4 5), and which then serve as the basic building blocks" of a drawing and that "could provide a scaffold that allowed others to learn, to teach and how to use the language."[3]

In other words, these twelve symbols act like letters in the words we call icons or images in visual thinking. Like letters make up words, these "letters" can be used together to create any image. The better we are at seeing images in these symbols in our imaginations, the easier it is to doodle them.

Next, I learned about something called "Elements of Sketchnoting." Sketchnotes are "a form of Visual Writing by expressing ideas, concepts, and important thoughts in a meaningful flow" with typography, dividers, connectors, containers, structure, and icons "by listening, processing, and transfer-

---

[3] Gray, Dave. "In Defense of the Visual Alphabet." Medium. January 13, 2017. https://medium.com/the-xplane-collection/in-defense-of-the-visual-alphabet-a8dcca7cf151.

ring what you hear by sketching either by analog or digital."[4] Each of these elements adds a different piece to a sketchnote and has a different job.

First, there is typography. Think fonts, and fonts on visual steroids. Typography dictates how we write the words. It is bold vs. regular, cursive vs. block lettering, swirls vs. straight. It can show importance, organize information, emphasize major ideas, and show the mood.

Next, there are dividers, arrows, and connectors. These marks show relationships among ideas and/or concepts. They connect ideas, pieces of stories, help show direction, and show visual sequence.

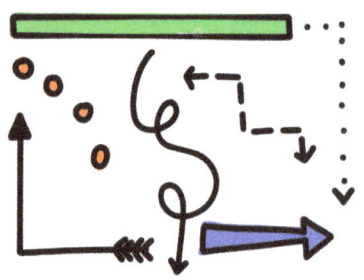

Containers are shapes that hold words. They can sort, give structure, show hierarchy, anchor information, provide structure, or be used to categorize information.

---

4   Thorn, Kevin. "Home." Nuggethead Studioz. September 03, 2013. http://nuggethead.net/2013/09/sketchnote-school-6-steps-to-great-conference-sketchnotes/.

Then there is the structure of a sketchnote. This is how we lay out and plan our sketchnote. Structures come in many shapes and styles and can be affected by the topic and/or by the sketchnoter/visual thinker's learning strengths and weaknesses.

Icons are the simple objects and images drawn to show what we are imagining.

I couldn't stop learning about visual note-taking and sketchnoting, visual thinking, visual writing, and all its bits and facets and pieces. I couldn't stop drawing. The happiness made my heart just explode.

But something was wrong.

Even with all this fantastic learning, with all these incredible experiences, with all of this happiness…it still hadn't happened.

"Why not?" it nudged.

That voice again.

"This is all great stuff, but are you ever going to bring it into your classroom?" it nagged.

"When are you going to try it with your students?" it shouted.

"They can't possibly sketchnote," I argued back.

"It's so fun. It makes you so happy," it reminded me.

"My students will never understand how to do it," I fought back. "And their fine motor skills. There is a reason we use assistive technology with them," I added.

The voices never let down and wouldn't stop. It suddenly became so powerful, so loud and so relentless.

There was incredible power in the kind of thinking and in the process I was experiencing. How long could I go on ignoring it all? How long would I go on pushing away this voice and the power I knew this learning and its experiences had? How long could I silence this voice that shouted at me, that reminded me…that knew?

THE PENCIL WAS WRITE….

With a lot of deep breathing, self-talk, trust in that inner voice, in all the research, and in my teacher's intuition, I dragged myself kicking and screaming. I stood in front of my class. It was a class of all boys. It was one of the hardest, most challenging classes of students, and the group who stretched every part of what I had ever learned in eighteen years of teaching. "Now is the time," the voice whispered.

I stood in front of my ELA class. My inner deep breathing was on overdrive. I shared with them what I had been learning. I shared my experiences, my new knowledge, and I told them it was something I just had to share with them. We were going to give it a try. I stood there, gulp, and they looked back at me.

> **The time, the group, the moment will never be perfect but this, what you will be sharing, teaching, giving them, it will forever make an impact.**

"Let's get out our books and open to our new story, 'The House of Usher.'"

I read the first paragraph out loud to them.

"What do you imagine when I read that?"

Silence.

"What movie is playing in your head?"

Not a word, not a raised hand…nothing.

I summoned all of my learning and experience.

"I imagine a man with wavy hair and wrinkles standing in a room in a robe," I shared. I turned toward my whiteboard and drew what I imagined.

"Draw what you imagine," I directed, and all of them copied exactly what I had drawn.

As I walked around the classroom, I smiled and commented on what I noticed about their doodles (er, what they had copied).

Weeks went by. Paragraph by paragraph we would read, and I would repeat, "What do you imagine when I read that? What movie is playing in your head?"

The silence continued.

Not a word.

I continued to share what I was imagining, doodling it on the board, and they would copy it in their books.

Then it happened.

One ELA period while I walked around, I noticed it.

CJ had decided not to doodle what I had.

His hand covered the doodle as I got closer.

"Let me see." I smiled.

He didn't budge.

I reminded him of the words I'd shared, "Ideas, not art. I want to see your imagination."

He slowly moved his hand to reveal a doodle that was nothing like the one I had doodled. His head hung down.

"Oh, my gawsh! That's fantastic, CJ! Tell me about it," I squealed.

I stood there with a smile I could not stop as he shared with me his visualizing and his connections to the text and the doodle.

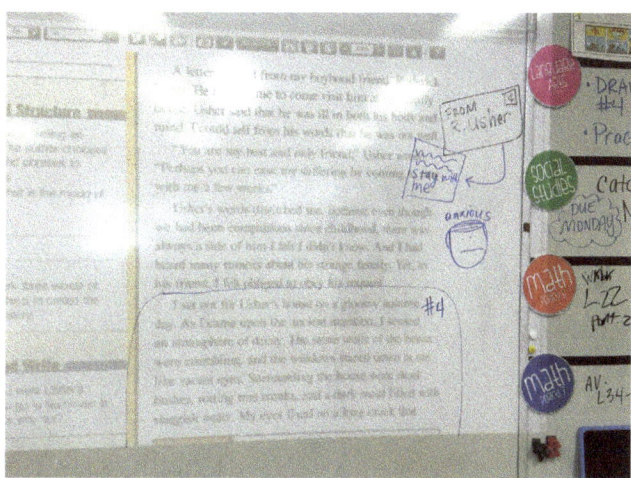

In that single instant, that single moment of what I like to call "the moment CJ went rogue," everything changed.

In that single instant, everyone's doodles became their own.

Now when I asked, "What do you imagine when I read that? What movie is playing in your head?" our classroom was filled with vivid and detailed images describing connections to the literature. Visuals filled their pages. Visuals fueled our discussions. Our learning conversations were richer and moved faster. My students were not only visualizing their reading, but they were also using the visuals to aid in their recall. Retention was deeper and information

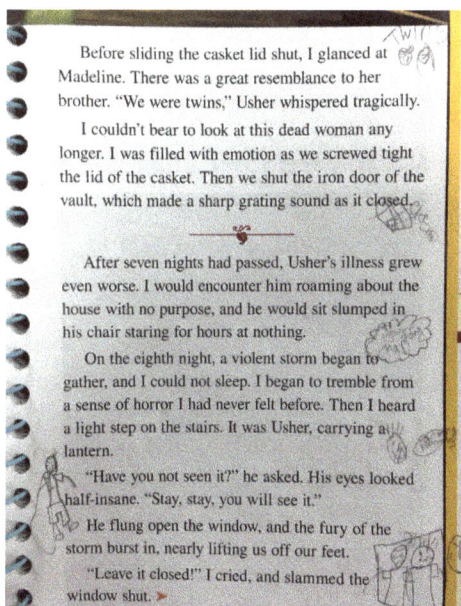

and learning were both easier to access. And at this moment, I learned a lesson I never expected I would need to learn.

OUR PENCIL WAS WRITE...
You see, it wasn't that my students couldn't visualize. It wasn't that they had a disability, had a language impairment, or didn't have the skills to think in pictures, that they weren't capable of this type of thinking, or that they were incapable of doodling. You see, it was me. I had let labels, cognitive levels, behaviors, previous experiences, and academic levels lie to me and doubt their potential.

It was never that they couldn't. It was that I had never given them a chance. I had never given them a chance to try. I never gave them a chance to succeed. I didn't give them a chance to learn it their way. I never gave them a chance to create their own rules. I never took a chance to stretch my own skills to meet their needs. I never took that chance to leap, to change everything, to break mindsets, to show all of us we can do it!

This experience blew me away, stopped me in my tracks, and changed my mindset all at once. Experiences, words, and time are powerful parts of what we bring to life, to our classrooms, and to the things we decide to try. Like my experiences with drawing and my mindset about bringing sketchnoting into my classroom, the thought of drawing, putting pencil to paper, stops us, freezes us, and keeps us from moving forward.

For you, that means it is time for you to start learning and experiencing too.

For some of you, my story is your story too. You can't remember liking to draw, and when you do draw, well, your drawings look like a five-year-old drew them. For others, you can't remember a time when doodling in the margins of your notebooks in school didn't happen. Heck, I bet you remember getting in trouble for it! And for others, still, you have always loved drawing and creating. This love has always been with you.

> When was the last time you remember drawing?

> When was the last time you remember LIKING to draw?

> How does having to draw make you feel?

> What do you think of others who can draw?

Still, others on our journeys into drawing are filled with emotion and very definitive feelings. Some of us feel so deeply and so strongly, "I CAN'T draw!" Somewhere in your life, someone (maybe yourself, maybe an adult from your childhood) told you something very, very specific and highly critical about your drawing and its worthlessness. You stopped drawing and haven't looked back. There are so many paths we can take to becoming a visual thinker and a learner who doodles. Each of our journeys is unique.

Let's start learning about yours. What your experiences hold and what the next step is for you in your doodling and drawing to learn journey.

To my fellow Five-Year-Old Doodlers: we draw like a five-year-old because the last time we drew was when we were five years old. Maybe we were asked what that doodle looked like and hung our head in shame or stopped drawing when others could not tell what we had drawn. No matter how happy doodling and drawing made us or how proud we were, it was only connected to others' opinions of it. We are instantly defensive about the thought of drawing.

Pssst, there is a ton of hope for us! Really! We didn't forget how to draw. We just forgot we could. There is an incredible visual thinker and doodler just waiting to be remembered and brought out!

To my amazing and incredible Closet Doodlers: say hello and introduce yourself to your inner awesome. Your journey is often filled with emotion as well. Shame, embarrassment, or a feeling that there is no one else out there like you. Do you remember doodling in the margin of your notebook? Remember being told to put your pencil down and to pay attention? Your teachers and/or parents all thought you were just spacing out. Dude, you were sketchnoting!

To the glorious, brave, and fearless Forever Doodlers: the ones who never let go of their love and their knowledge of their inner drawer, their inner creator. Drawing and creating has always brought you joy. No one could make you feel or think you were different. You've known all along, haven't you? You've never silenced the feelings drawing brought you. You know the strength of doodling and drawing and all the happiness they bring.

And to you. No, I did not forget about you. To those of you who believe to your core I Can't Draw: You say to others, "Have you seen me draw a line? Ha! It isn't even straight!" Your history with drawing runs long and deep, and you definitely don't remember it ever being fun. You will flatter me and keep reading. Heck, you will even do the activities below and even learn. Learn for your students or your children. All the while you will think, "See, I told you, Carrie! Deal with it! I am not a drawer. I cannot draw…end of story!"

So, what type of doodler are you? *(Circle one. Yes, it's okay to write in this book.)*

Seriously, dude. I Can Not Draw.
My Inner Doodler is a Five-Year-Old.
I'm a Closet Doodler.
I'm a Forever Doodler.

Whether you look at the floor and strongly declare, "I cannot draw," haven't connected with your inner doodler since you were five years old, have been a closet doodler afraid to unleash your love of it into the world, or are a longtime lover of all things doodlie, each of our paths are important. Each of us brings very special, deeply personal, and powerful experiences. All of these experiences are full of valuable knowledge and a new power to connect with ourselves. Through these experiences we can empower ourselves and our students to connect with visual thinking and doodling to learn.

You have just met your inner doodler and it is incredible!

I told you it was in there!

Each of our journeys gives us a starting point, insight, and a direction that points where to go next. There is great value in our stories. Our stories are each filled with unique experiences and lessons. Our journeys gift us rich understanding, valuable insight into ourselves, and a special and unique connection with the future visual thinkers and doodlers we will meet.

Becoming a visual thinker and a learner who doodles does not come without a leap. For some, it is a small step or a shift in our thinking. For others, still, it is the biggest leap we have taken and it's absolutely terrifying. Whether it is a step or a leap, it is something you have to take to become a visual thinker and intentional doodler. It has to be done to be ready to connect with our learners, to be ready to share this skill with others, to tap into this incredible part of you, and to be able to take our learners on their own journeys. To do this, you have to pick up a pencil (okay, your favorite pen will work great too) and start to draw.

I promise, your pencil is so, so, so ready!

So, take a breath. Tell yourself, "I got this."

Take some time.

Remember what you have learned so far.

Remember your inner doodler you met earlier.

Let's take some time to really get to know what your inner doodler needs. Let's also get to know the feelings this experience can bring us (and our students). Give yourself permission to take what you have learned, to be the visual thinker and doodler you are, and give yourself permission to do it your way, at your pace, and with your feelings. Connecting with and knowing the feelings that our experiences bring us will allow us to better connect with the learners we will connect with.

My Inner Doodler is a Five-Year-Old: Cannot remember the last time you drew. You use phrases like, "I draw like a five-year-old."

"I can barely draw a stick figure!"

"Ha! I can't draw!"

"Ugggg! This is so frustrating!"

I'm a Closet Doodler: Have always loved to doodle and secretly drew in the margins, filled up notebooks, drew on napkins, on worksheets. You say things like, "I've always done that."

"This is so me!"

"I got in trouble for doing this in school."

I am a Forever Doodler: Have always believed in your drawing abilities. When you draw in class, you know you totally got this. You talk about drawing and doodling, using words like, "I can draw that!"

"I'll draw!"

"This is fun."

"I love this!!"

I Can't Draw: Tricky ones. You're certain and definitive and totally sure, "I cannot draw."

It's happening.

Yep, it is.

Pencil ready!

The year was 2016 and the Chicago Cubs won the World Series. Cubs fever could not be ignored, especially in a middle school in the northwest suburbs of Chicago. It was the same year I had Mary in my class. Mary definitively and with absolute certainty said, "I cannot, CANNOT draw." Now, I had met "I can't draw" doodlers before, but Mary was the most certain, absolutely and totally certain "I can't draw," no-budging student I had ever had. There was just no way I was changing this eighth-grade girl's mind.

"I Can't Draw" doodlers are a unique breed. Their certainty is a wall they hide behind. Their beliefs are rooted in experiences and words like, "I can't draw," "I can't remember the last time someone said something nice about my drawing," "My straight lines aren't even straight," "I'm a terrible artist," "I can't remember ever thinking something nice when I drew." These words are married to deep-rooted feelings of sadness, judgment, shame, and sometimes pain. They are tricky because it is not just moments that have created this wall. Their wall was created brick by brick and cemented in uncertainty, negative thoughts, and the unkind, judgmental, or thoughtless words of others.

It's time to tear it down!

Let's start by seeing what your wall is made of.

1. What do you remember about drawing? Write it in the box. "I remember…"
2. Label that cement with experiences you remember about drawing.
3. Fill those bricks in with the feelings you have when you think about drawing or doodling.

the i cant wall

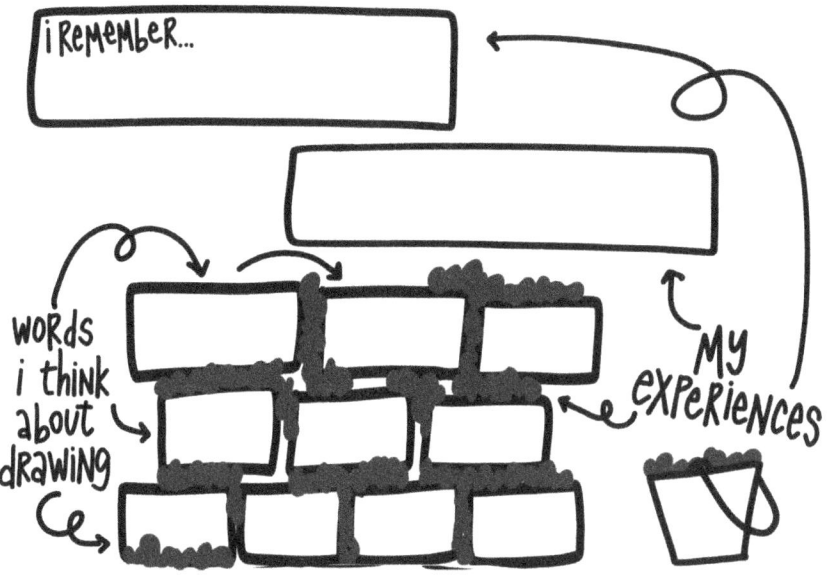

Giving up is not a place I come to easily. With Mary, I had a choice. I could accept her words and move on, or I could decide I was going to teach her she could. There was no getting around Mary's certainty. No amount of sweet-talking, just try it, I'll show you how, or we-can-try-it-togethers worked (seriously, peeps, the "I can't" power is strong). So, I came up with a plan. It was a plan that involved **experiences, words, and time**. First, I would make sure Mary experienced visual thinking and doodling to learn without the drawing part. I would create experiences that would make her feel safe. Let her feel what it was like to be part of a classroom that accepted all types and levels of doodlers. During these experiences I would fill her with new words, help her create a new dialogue in her head, and give her a new doodling mantra. I would rebuild her mindset.

Now that we have talked about that wall of yours, like Mary, it is time to fill yourself up with experiences and new words. Let's start rebuilding that mindset.

Experiences

Life is jam-packed full of moments that are just waiting for a doodle to be added to it.

These moments offer our doodlers opportunities to dip their toes into doodling and rebuild and strengthen their walls and mindset.

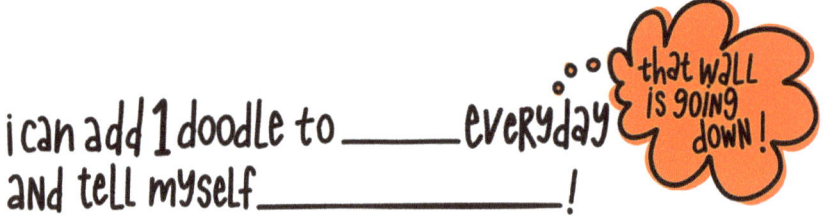

Life, experiences, learning, and moments are just waiting to be scribbled into doodles. From adding a doodle to our favorites list, a to-do list, events on your calendar, a recipe, when you write directions, the directions of a DIY project, your family chores, a staff meeting note, or added to your kid's lunch note, each of these everyday activities are an experience that can help us chip away at that wall.

Pick up a pencil and add doodles to a piece of your life. Doodle by doodle, give yourself experiences and words that will strengthen and encourage your drawing.

Words

Now let's pair these experiences with the words. These words will help you chip at and crush that wall.

Your Inner Doodler is a Five-Year-Old: Let each experience remind you of what you can do, what moments of drawing you have stepped into and tried. Yeah, you! Then give yourself more words to remind you of the awesome thing you are doing. Then give yourself time and lots of experiences.

Closet Doodler: Give yourself permission. Give yourself permission to draw, to feel, to be happy, and permission not to

hide this creative part of you. Smile and hold your pencil high and proudly say, "I love doodling and drawing!" Then put your pencil to paper and draw, and draw, and draw some more and remind yourself it is okay for this to make you happy.

Forever Doodler: This is your chance to take your inner drawer, wrap it in a huge hug, and hold on to it tight. It is your chance to take this experience and add it to the passion drawing already brings you. Dive into all of this and make it your own.

Time

Just in case more bricks need to be broken or that wall needs just a little more time to fall…it doesn't mean you're a lost cause. Take a look at your world and think about your daily routine or that list of ideas from above. Where can we add more images to our thinking and our life? Just because I gave you permission to think differently doesn't mean you (or I) are giving up on that inner doodler. This is your permission to give yourself time. Time to have more experiences and time to fill yourself up with new words.

HER PENCIL WAS WRITE… After months of experiences, words shared over, and over, and over again to remind Mary of the incredible thinker and visualizer she is, after moments spent together with our class learning, thinking, and imagining together, Mary did it. One morning during fourth-period Social Studies, the class was sitting on the floor. We were gathered around a long piece of white butcher paper writing facts about the end of World War II. As we added to the butcher paper, our heads were down with a marker in hand. We all worked together to combine our learning with doodles of the words we imagined.

"I did it!" we suddenly heard.

"I did it!" Mary said louder.

I looked up from a doodle I had added with the other students to see Mary had gone rogue. She had added her own part. With her purple glitter-painted nail, she pointed at a navy-lined rectangle with a capital blue "W" in the center.

You see, Mary knew the allies had won World War II. She also knew just what winning looks like. It looks like the Chicago Cubs "W" flag.

"I can draw, Mrs. Baughcum! I can draw!" Mary shouted through her smile, and at that moment, her experiences, new words, and time had taken down her "I Can't Wall," and she never ever looked back!

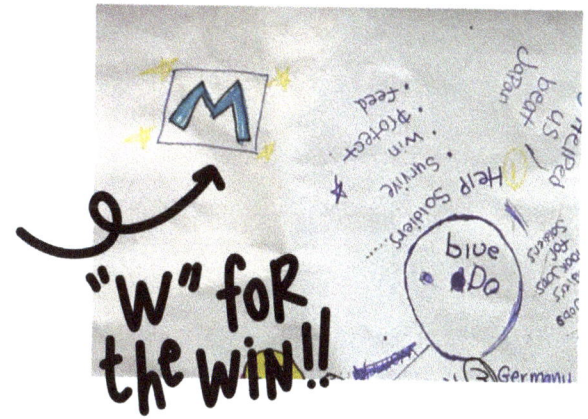

Part 3: VISUALIZE

It happened on a Saturday. We both woke early to go and connect, be inspired by, and share moments with other educators. All it took was a moment and a schedule board at an Edcamp. She had been invited to live sketchnote the opening of Edcamp Chicago. I was there because, well, it's an Edcamp and umm… I love them. Giggles, bagels, introduction, hugs (dude I am a total hugger… so watch out) and morning coffee happened. Ben got things started and she captured everything he said in a wonderful and perfectly captured visual display of everything that makes Edcamp wonderful. Each year my children get a chance to go to one Edcamp with me. This one was the one Tei picked. They stood with me and proposed our session idea. I couldn't wait to talk all things sketchnotes with anyone who would listen. After the intro and schedule building, I walked up to the live sketchnoter and introduced myself. I couldn't say enough about all that she had just created. Such an amazing creative mind.

"We should do the sketchnoting session together," I said.

She smiled and was in…even if I had to drag her.

The morning came, went, lunch, pizza, side-aching giggles over lunch, and then the afternoon. The final session of the day came and the live sketchnoter and I were ready to talk and share our passion for visuals to all who would listen. Caught up in the moment, we whispered and quickly planned together in the front of the room. When we looked up, the room was overflowing with others sitting, standing, and watching from the hallway. In that moment, two educators with a common passion shared their very different paths into sketchnoting, effortlessly bouncing ideas off each other, ideas flowing from the room, sharing inspiration, lessons, activities, passion, doodles...lots of doodles and laughs.

In this single moment, a Saturday in April, two educators found each other. Two very different sketchnoters were forever connected. That Saturday, two women found an incredible friendship. Two kindred creators...two sketchnote soul mates found each other, destined to be forever connected and forever kindred spirits.

Her name was Dana Ladenburger.

From the moment we shared our ideas at an Edcamp, we knew that the two of us together was something very, very special. Something that could not be denied or ignored. We not only knew the power of visual thinking and the doodle, we also knew the power of our two passions combined. Our moment at Edcamp could not be ignored. Dana and I could not wait to talk, to create together, and to take what we had found in each other and use its power to share with others the power of sketchnoting.

Text after text, getting to know each other, we knew this was something more than special. We knew this was kismet. We knew we had to make what we had something that others could learn from and something others could infuse their classrooms with too. A workshop proposal accepted by our state conference was just the fuel we needed.

Sunday after Sunday we woke before sunrise to drive to a Panera halfway between the two of us. We spent hour after hour talking all things visualizing, doodles, and sketchnoting. Dana and I knew the power of visuals just couldn't be denied. From board games to movie ads, to the YouTube videos our students watch and Instagram, but visuals also go back to the beginning of time—the cave men and Egyptians. Visuals are timeless. Visuals are language-less, they grab our attention, they make information stick, they improve our communication, they enhance our thinking, and they make complex language understandable. Fueled by this incredible new connection, our Sunday conversations and my going rogue classroom moment, each social studies, reading, math lesson—heck any lesson I planned—became an opportunity for me to develop my students' visual thinking skills. Each lesson was an experience for them to put pencil to paper and doodle their learning. My view of information and how learners processed (or didn't process) information visually was changed forever. I was hungry to learn more about it and how I could develop, create, and strengthen this incredible skill in my students.

David Gray, author of *Game Storming: A Playbook for Innovators, Rule Breakers and Changemakers* and xplaner.com says, "Visual thinking is a way to organize your thoughts and improve your ability to think and communicate. It's a great way to convey complex or potentially confusing information." When we look at all the organizational tools and processes we have available to us, heck, it's like looking at the history of teaching and note-taking lessons. Mind Mapping, Graphic Organizers, Storyboarding, Brainstorming, Simple Sketch, Problem Solving, Reveal Process all have powerful elements within them that connect to a variety of learners' strengths and pair well with specific tasks. The single most powerful element each of these organizational tools lack is visuals…pictures, drawing, doodles…visual connections from the mind to the hand to the pencil onto the paper. The single most simple addition with huge impact that could be added to any of these tools is visuals…pictures, drawing, doodles…visual connections from the mind to the hand to the pencil onto the paper. When ideas and information are connected to images and then drawn, they have enormous effect on retention, comprehension, recall and attention.

> there is no this way, no it is only called this, no there is only one purpose for, no one style, no one subject, no one strategy, no one way…

I say all of this because I believe to my core the power of learning to visualize, to visualizing, to teaching visualizing, to bringing visual thinking into your world. You only need to know, believe, understand, and to own to your core the power visuals and visual thinking contain. Your imagination, the movie that plays in your head and the connections those visuals make to information and ideas, in any form, in any style, no matter what it is called, no matter how it is organized, no matter what the topic, no matter what our age, is powerful.

So how can we build this skill? How can we remind students it is there? How can we make it a continued practice layered over learning and our teaching?

It all starts by remembering it is already there.

We take in information with our eyes or our ears, we process the information and decide what we understand vs what we do not, connect it to what we already know, and we visualize (see a picture in our head) the information.

Visualizer's Mantra: What movie is playing in your head?
What picture do you imagine when you hear _____?
What picture is in your head? What do you see when you think of _____?

So what the heck does that even look and sound like? How do we even get started?

Well, pick a subject.

Yep, any subject.

Pick a moment.

Yep, any moment.

Nope, doesn't matter.

Share what you have been learning about right here. Share out loud with your students what you are thinking about when you teach. Share with them why this is important to do when we are learning.

Yes, seriously.

Then tell them exactly what you are visualizing:

"When I hear this/read that, the movie playing in my head is _____. The picture I imagine is _____."

Say in words describing (out loud) exactly what you are imagining in your head. Tell them what it is, what it looks like in your brain, what it feels like and how it happens. Tell them why they should care (remember, good comprehenders visualize when they are learning).

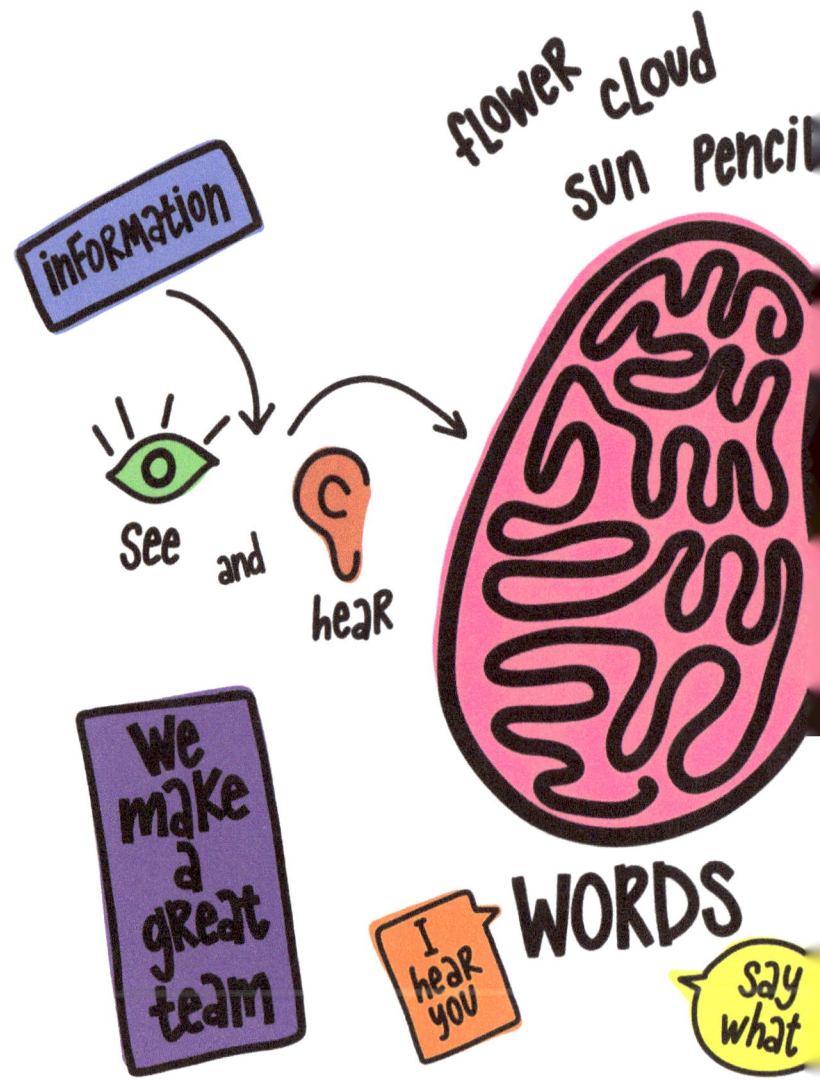

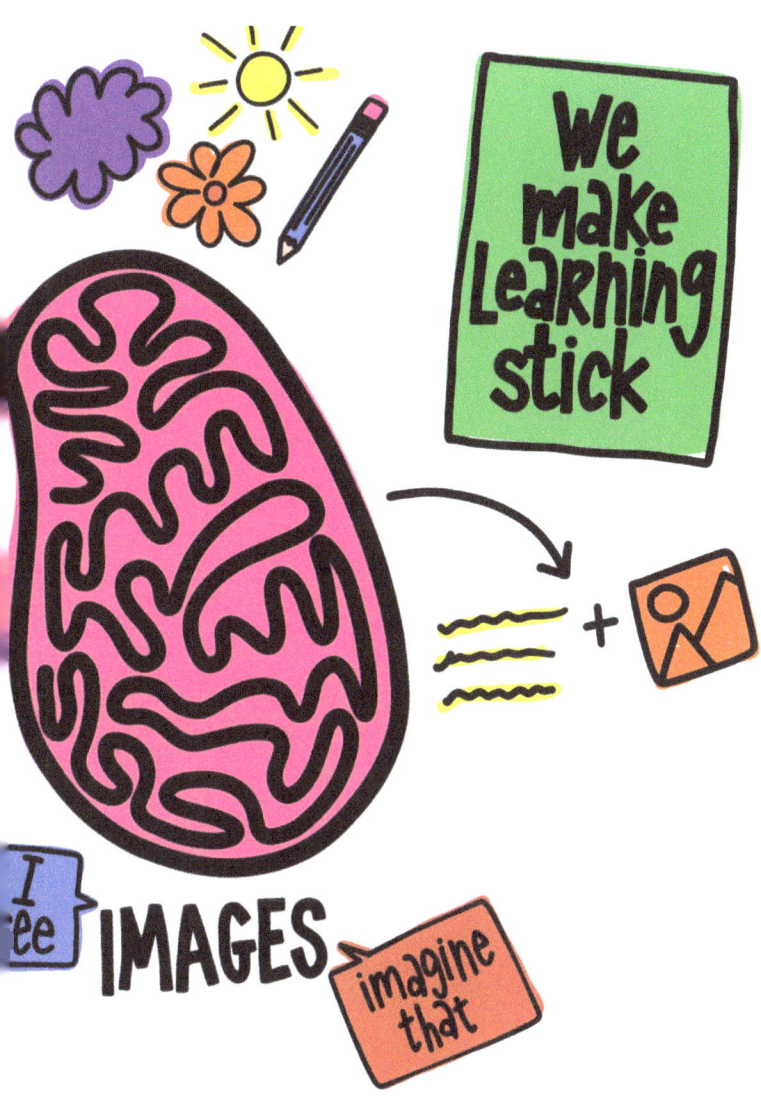

Make visualizing and visual thinking expected. Expect visualizing every day with every lesson and in all the moments.

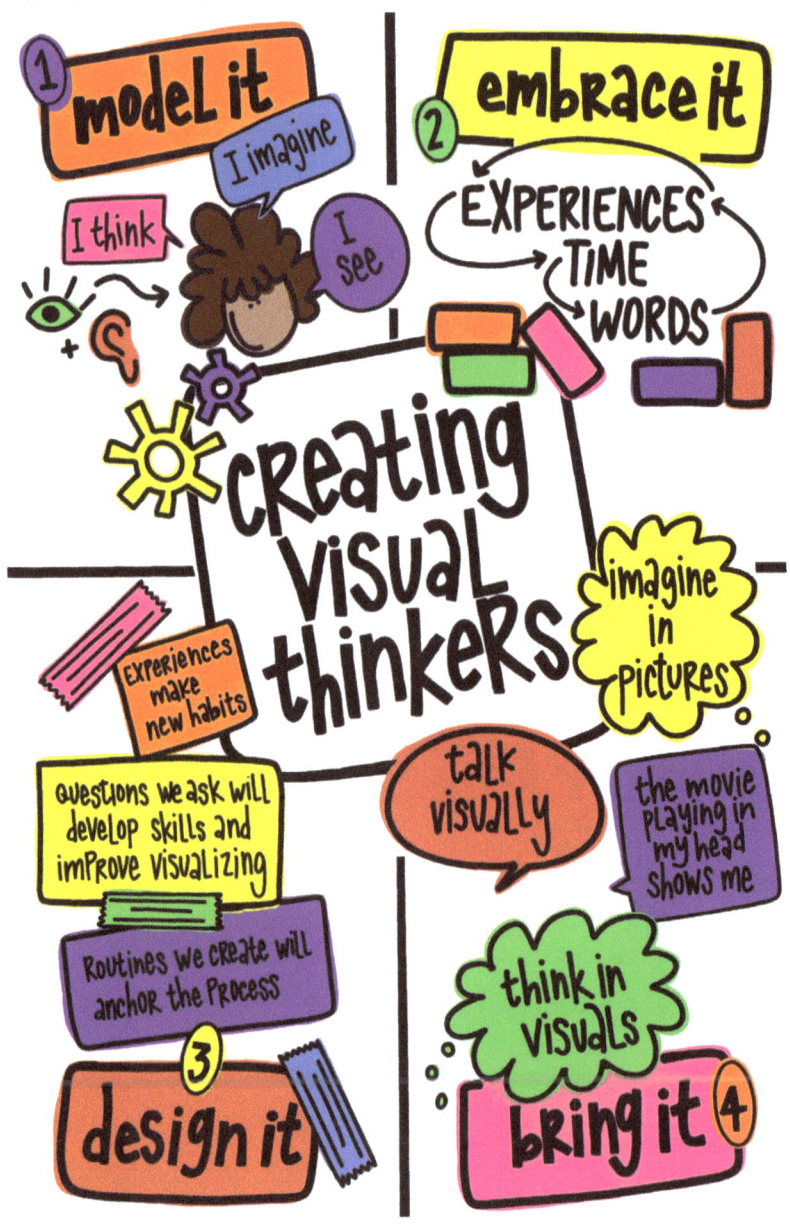

Creating Visual Thinkers

It should not be assumed that all of our students are automatically visual thinkers. For some, it will be something that comes naturally, that has always been a part of how their minds work. For others, they will just need to be reminded, "Oh yeah! That happens in my brain and I should pay attention to it." For others, visual thinking is a skill that is not there or needs further development. Regardless of where we fall on that continuum of visualizing skills (*note: our ability to visualize is not correlated with our ability to draw*), modeling visual thinking, activating visual thinking, creating visual thinking habits and routine, and "seeing" visuals will have a powerful effect on improving how all of us understand the world around us.

Modeling Visual Thinking

Share your thinking. When information comes in or is read, verbalize what is happening in your mind. Verbally share what movie is playing in your imagination, what picture is in your head, and allow your students to hear, see, and experience how visualization feels and happens:

"When I read _____, it makes me imagine _____."
"When I hear the author say _____, the movie playing in my head is _____."
"I imagine _____."
"I see _____ when I hear/read _____."
"The movie in my head shows me _____."

My Pencil Made Me Do It

The visual thinking routine you create will anchor the process, solidify it, and maximize its potential for use. Make visualizing questions and language an expectation in all learning. The questions you ask during learning experiences will develop and improve visualizing.

Questions to activate visual thinking:

what
"What do you imagine _____ looks like?"
"What do you imagine _____ means?"
"What do you imagine happens?"
"What do you imagine when I ask you _____?"
"What do you see in your imagination that makes you say that?"
"What do those words make you picture?"
"What images do those words give you?"
"Tell me more about what you are picturing in your head?"
"What are you imagining that supports that answer?"
"What does that make you imagine?"
"What images do those words give you?"
"What do you imagine will happen next?"

how
"Explain to me with pictures from your imaginations how _____ _____?"
"How does _____ look?"

when
"When _____ happens, what do you imagine?"
"When _____ stated _____, what did that make you imagine?"
"When you imagine _____, _____, and _____, what does that all mean?"
"When _____, _____, and _____ happens, what do you imagine will happen next?"

Why "Why does _____ make us imagine _____?"
"Help me see what you are thinking by describing it with words."
"These words make me imagine _____."

Create Visual Thinking Habits

Visual thinkers are created like doodlers: with experiences, time, and words. We can begin to do this by first understanding our own visual thinking strengths, weaknesses, and habits. It starts by thinking about how we visualize and how we build those skills.

Think of your brain as a warehouse of visual knowledge. A warehouse organized into two sections: the knowledge library section and the icon library section. The knowledge section organizes its information in boxes, while the icon section organizes by item. When we are little, the boxes in our knowledge section are small, and there are not very many of them. Our boxes are still small because they are waiting to grow and be filled with information. The icon section of our warehouse is jam packed full of icons busting at the seams because we have not lost our love for drawing. Images are language-less, and images are how we show our learning and communicate our ideas. As adults, the knowledge section of our warehouse grows. Some boxes get bigger, holding more information on topics, others might shrink, and still others are added each time we learn something new. The icon section of our warehouse may hold only a few dusty, forgotten icons, or it may be hidden and forgotten. No matter. Its shelves are endless and waiting to be filled. Each time a new icon is doodled, it is added to its "I know how to draw that" shelves.

This library, this warehouse, as I like to call it, is a visual thinker's and doodler's everything. The warehouse organizes and supplies us with the knowledge and holds the icons we know how to draw.

Now it is time to start connecting with and building your knowledge and icon library. Yes. You are ready. Let's do this!

Part 1

1. List five things you love, like, or are interested in: _____ _____
2. Rank their level of interest to you.
3. Add those words to boxes 1-5.

PaRt 2

1. Pick three things you want to learn more about: _____
   _____
2. Rank those by interest.
3. Add those words to the rest of the boxes (on page 63).

PaRt 3

Time to stock that icon library. Did you know it's already partially stocked? Really, it is! Think about what you have already learned!

1. Add those twelve visual alphabet shapes…you already know them.
2. Read a word from one of your boxes, imagine it in your head, and draw the images you imagine about the topic (use the visual alphabet to help you).

Your understanding will give you new tools to build visual thinkers. Time, life, practice and words will encourage this way of thinking and facilitate its development. Think out loud, ask questions, provide experiences, show, model, and expect visual thinking. Engage in these practices so often and with so many different activities that thinking with visuals becomes the norm. Give them experiences. Then be patient and use the power of time to allow the skill to develop at the learner's pace and with their experiences. Use your words to encourage and create a positive environment that will facilitate a world full of colorful, vivid, and powerful imaginations that see ideas and learning in pictures and movies.

Create a Visual Thinking Routine

Make the words and thinking present every day and with all information: "We take in information, connect it to what we know, and imagine/play a movie of it in our head. What movie does that make you play in your head?"

MY PENCIL WAS WRITE… After months spent learning as much as I could about visualizing, how we imagine the movie or image in our heads, practicing, stretching my thinking, creating, teaching and learning more ways to get others imagining and doodling, and then doodling and doodling some more, it didn't take long before visuals were everywhere in my classroom. It wasn't long before visual thinking became a language in my class. When

I asked questions to check for comprehension, I did not just ask who-what-when questions anymore. I started by asking students to tell me what they imagined. When we talked and learned about a subject, I rephrased questions so they required visualizing to answer. No matter the task or the subject, visual thinking became ever-present.

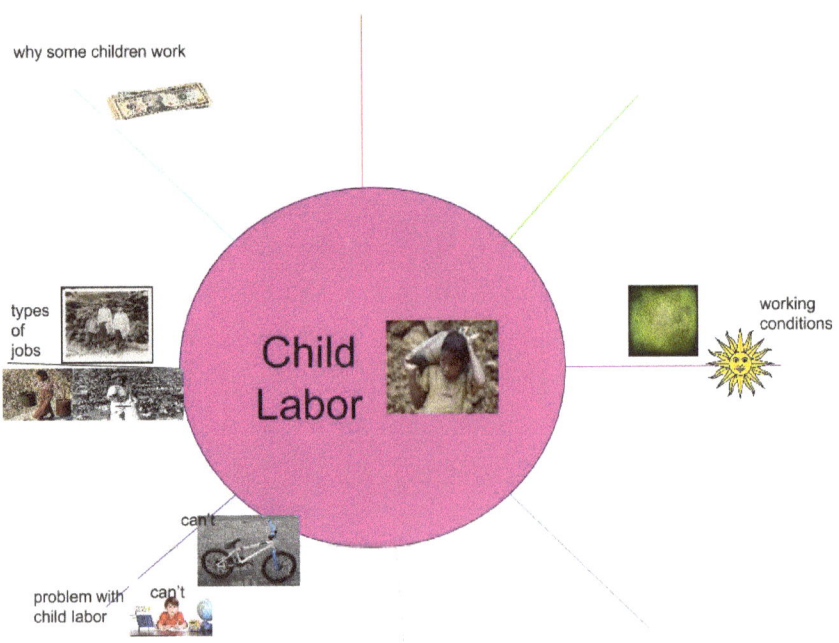

We drew in margins of books, on the whiteboard, on paper, Post-its, note cards—well, we drew everywhere and on everything because everything had changed. Our thinking had changed, our mindset had changed, how we learned had changed, and how I taught them had changed. With each new doodle, each new lesson, each new day, each new moment, these experiences and our thinking were becoming so ingrained that visualizing was instantaneous. The images were in their brains as soon as the words and information connected with them...and it was awesome!

With the "I can't draw" walls torn down, and visualizing learning being exercised daily, I knew they were ready to start upping their visual thinking game. Only now it was time for them to take those single images and learn to combine them with words and other images. It was time to learn to synthesize and add the words they heard/read to the images they imagined. To do this, I decided to start with a structured approach. An approach that would enable them to compensate for language weaknesses while teaching them how to add new thinking skills to the skills they already had. After years of struggling with language and being taught traditional notetaking, I would need to meet them where they were at, but also provide the support they would need. I needed them to take in, understand, and organize large quantities of information they were hearing, seeing, or reading, and take written notes on it.

And I'll bet my students aren't the only ones this is hard for: Try sitting next to someone at a conference during a session or keynote and try to keep them from talking in excitement from all the new and important learning. You too? Try sitting through an entire science lesson on the chemical properties of matter thinking, *oh, I will remember this*, only to get home and realize you have forgotten everything your teacher said in class. You too? Try reading the assigned chapter in *The Outsiders* only to get to class the next day and not take enough notes on what you read or on the right information. You too? So it isn't just my students?

I started the lesson. I instructed them to take notes on any information about D-Day. If the information was on-topic, new, important,

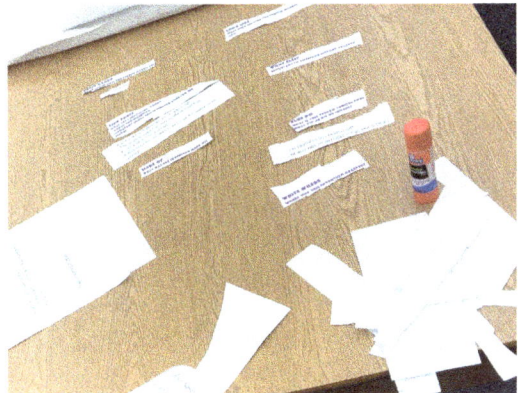

or made them feel something, they should type it. Students listened to information for thirty seconds to a minute, then I would pause and students would type their notes. I repeated any part of the information if a student asked. We repeated this process until the entire lesson was done. With a final instruction to review their facts and make sure they were only about D-Day, they printed their traditional-style notes. Next I asked them to cut out the facts into strips. With a long piece of white butcher block paper I spread out on a table, it was time to organize the facts and start micro-summarizing.

When we read or listen to information and take notes traditionally by hand or with technology, large amounts of information are captured. Notes are taken without a lot of synthesis or connecting to the information. When we micro-summarize, we take information, connect it to what we know, and synthesize the information into a phrase or simple sentence, forcing us to think about our thinking, what we want to learn and are learning.

When we learn, we take in information with our eyes or our ears, we process the information, and we decide what we understand versus what we do not. Then we create questions to seek more information, or we connect it to what we already know, transform the information into a more concise and meaningful phrase, and connect that information to the image we visualize with it.

So at this point you may be thinking, *OK, Carrie, I get what you are saying so far. I even agree with you. Note-taking, synthesizing and summarizing information into our own words is a valuable skill for all of us to have, but have you seen how many note-taking strategies and tools there are out there?*

Yes, I have! There are tons. When it comes to visual thinking and doodle-making, we still face learners every day who have experienced a traditional education of taking notes in lists or pages, or strategies full of words. That means to shift from this ingrained thinking we need to give our learners words, give them new experiences, and take them on a new journey with their learning. So, what if we didn't disvalue other forms of notetaking but instead saw the strengths that each one contained? What if we looked at the unique elements each of them offers learners and layered it over and/or connected it to this new thinking? What if we started taking notes not only using our minds, but also considering how the information connects to our hearts?

It starts with each of us connecting with our own journey as notetakers. Yep, those "I can't" voices and experiences of doubt are everywhere. Even here with notetaking! From the "Yeah!! This I can do. I totally got this" notetakers to the "Please don't make me" notetakers, each notetaker, like learners and doodlers, comes with a variety of skills and experiences. Our journeys are equally unique. When it comes to taking notes and capturing information, which type of notetaker are you?

"Write All the Words" Notetaker: Type or write notes on all the things, capturing every word as much and as fast as you can.

"Bold is Gold" Notetaker: Take notes on what you're told to. Bullet points, bold print, and quotes make you think, *This must be important.*

"Sweet Spot" Notetaker: You know there are really only 3-5 important facts per page. You take notes on the essential facts and focus in on information that supports the subject/topic you are learning about.

"Taking Notes on a Feeling" Notetaker: You really have no idea what to take notes on. No strategy every really stuck with you. You type whatever feels important or what you are told to type. Sometimes it is what the person next to you is writing, or maybe you do not take any at all because, you know, "I'll remember this later. I don't need to write it down."

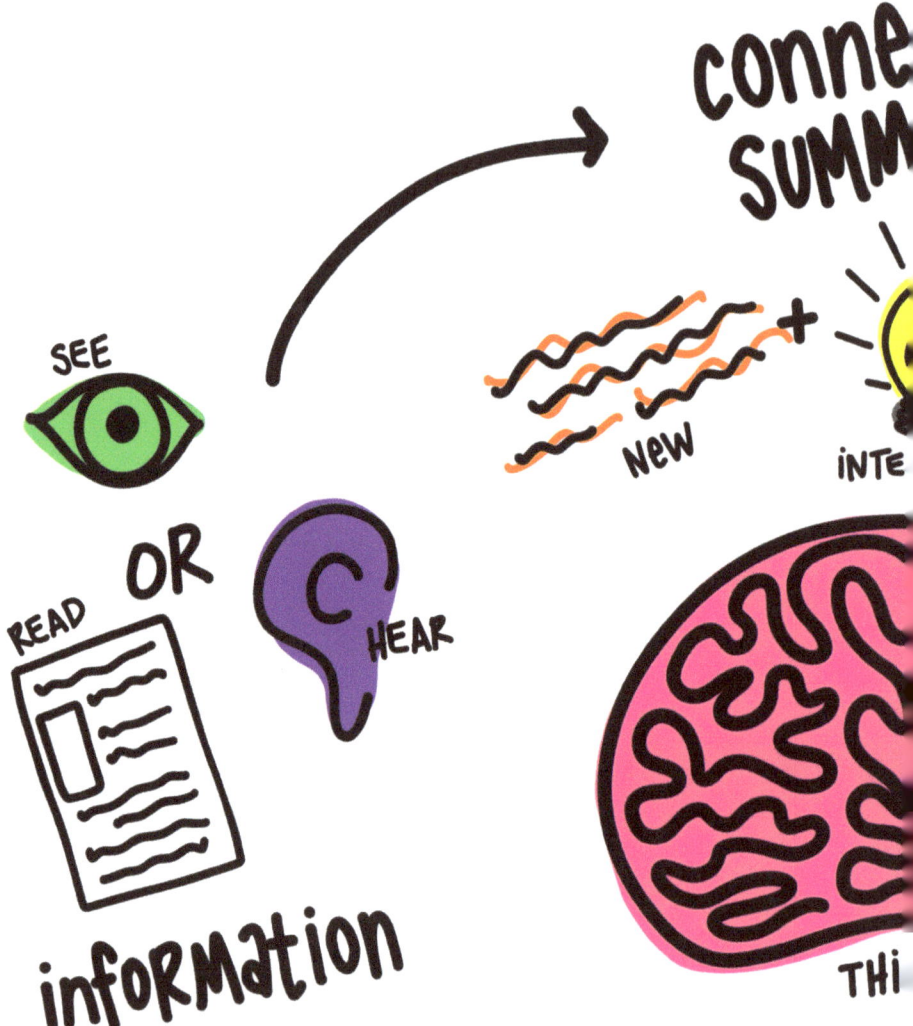

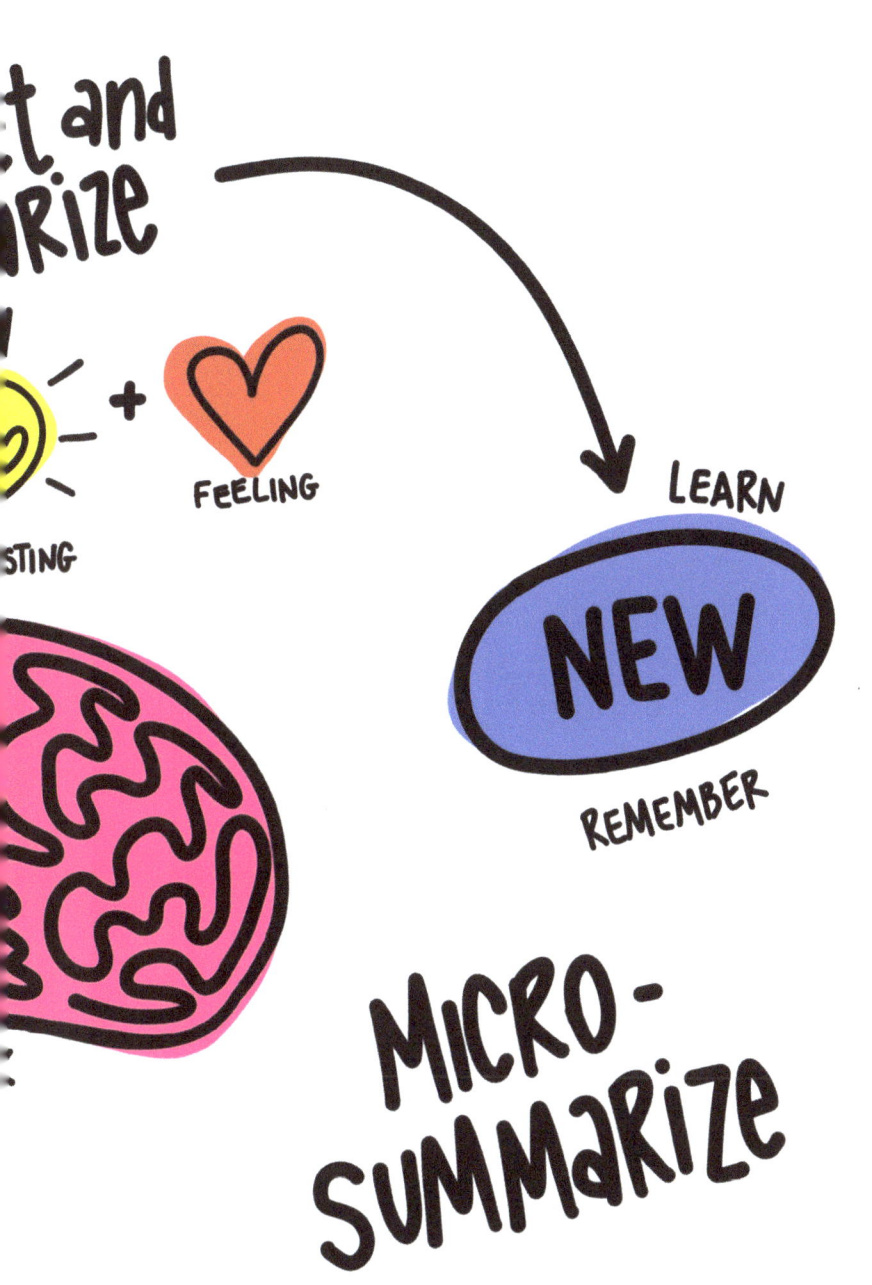

How do we learn to use this new way of thinking to enhance the strengths of our current methods? It starts just like building visualizing skills: developing your micro-summarizing skills by working with short, small pieces of information and then progressing toward larger, more lengthy chunks of information. What if, just like learning to visualize information, learning to micro-summarize came with its own verbal mantra…

Let's practice!

Take a look at this blog post…OK, it's a blog post about me. It's the story behind why I became a teacher. Thought I'd share a little bit more about me and let you get to know me a little better. And ooooo, bonus! You can work on your micro-summarizing.

MICRO-SUMMARIZING MANTRA:
Is it NEW? Is it INTERESTING?
Does it make you feel something?

1. Read this passage one paragraph at a time.
2. Use the margin to take notes.
3. Take notes on information that is new, interesting, or makes you feel something. *Side note: depending on the students I am working with, I will sometimes add, "Is it on topic?"*

Carrie Baughcum

MY STORY...WHY I BECAME A TEACHER

National Teacher Appreciation Week has filled my blog stream with all kinds of stories about teachers! Some stories have been about why they became teachers, others have been about what they learned from the teachers they had, and some have thanked the educators who have inspired them. Reading them made me smile. We don't just touch our students, but we have the chance every day to impact and inspire future educators and each other...but these posts also got me thinking. I have never shared my story. I have never shared why I became a teacher.

Here is my story...

I was so very proud to earn it. That neon-orange vinyl belt that went over my shoulder, around my waist. It clipped in the front and held my silver badge. I was a patrol. My first job as a patrol was to hold the stop sign as kids crossed the street (from what I recall, a pretty busy one), then higher powers realized it probably wasn't a good idea for a kid to do that, and an adult replaced us. So then I was given bus duty. My job was to monitor students getting off the bus and make sure they went to their classes. One day that bus came. It was the bus with the students in the special education classes. They were students with significant disabilities (what I would now describe as significantly cognitively impaired and significantly autistic students). I was curious and then eager to help. Every day I looked forward to an opportunity to assist those students from the bus to their classroom (a mobile classroom away from our school and in no way integrated...I know, but that was how it was) and back to the bus in the afternoon.

Throughout the school year my eagerness to help quickly grew into a fondness, a curiosity, and a desire to learn and do more with this teacher and her students. So when the school year ended, I decided I wanted to do more. (I must have talked to the teacher about this all on my own. I don't even remember how it all came together.) That summer I came to school every day during those students' summer school and helped. Each morning I woke up early, got on my bike, and rode it to my elementary school (yes, the ride was uphill, and it was a heck of a hill). I remember watching the teacher, studying her, and falling in love with everything that being a teacher to those students was. It was in those moments of that summer that I knew I wanted to be a teacher.

It was that summer that I discovered and knew that this is what I was made to do.

Since that moment in the mobile classroom between the school and the baseball fields, the teacher I have become has also been touched by other fantastic and truly inspiring teachers along the way. From my cooperating teacher during my student teaching, who taught me strategies and how to see the whole child, how to see the potential in each student, and how, if we work hard enough, every child can learn; to the associate principal who patiently gave me my first and most valuable lessons in behavior modification, point sheets, classroom structure, and motivating students when all I could do was make it through that ninth period class without letting my students see me cry (one of the toughest groups of kids I have ever had, and an experience I cherish deeply even to this day); to the principal who gave me new life when she trusted, valued, and respected my skills; and to the fellow educator who saved me from burnout and relit a passion that now burns stronger than it ever did before. ...It all started with those moments, that summer, in fifth grade.

Let's take a look at what you wrote in the margins.

 Are they all on topic? Does the information only talk about why I became a teacher? If it doesn't, cross it out.

 Is it new information to you? We do not need to write information we already know. The connections we make to the information and the image in our head will anchor already-known information. If it isn't, cross it out.

 Is it important? Assessing whether information is important to the topic will help us weed out unnecessary facts. If it isn't an important fact, cross it out.

 Does it make you feel something? Let's not dismiss the importance of information/learning that makes us feel something. Connecting information to a feeling anchors and solidifies our learning. When we feel something about a topic or lesson, learning it is more meaningful and we are more connected to it.

How many facts are left? Three to five-ish facts that were new, important, or made you feel something? Well, woohoo to you! Great job! You're a natural!

More than five-ish facts? Way more than five-ish facts? It's OK. Time to build those micro-summarizing skills.

Are any of them similar? Let's pair them up:

Now, think about what those facts have in common and combine the facts that are alike into one phrase.

...What did you say?

"But wait! I want to imagine these phrases and doodle the image from my head all at once," you say? I love how you think!

Now, breaking old habits is never easy. Sometimes a new way of thinking is all we need to change an old skill into a new one. Other times it is better to meet people (or ourselves) where skills are at, show and tell what they (we) are doing that is awesome, and then add small ideas or suggestions to refine skills.

I know, I know…I still haven't talked about how we are going to be able to listen, take in information, micro-summarize, and connect it with a doodle all at once. I will get there, I promise. Each skill has incredible strength on its own, and together they are even more powerful.

Ideas for Building Micro-Summarizing Capacity and Endurance

Ideas for Building Micro-Summarizing Experiences:

- **Topic-Idea Flood**: Take everything you learned about the topic and flood your paper with it. Then combine like facts (by color/container/icon) to create a summary.
- **Important Words**: Capture the important words from reading, scatter them on a paper, write them on Post-its or notecards, and use them to write a summary.
- **Type Notes, Cut Them Up**: Take notes using a computer/iPad, print them, cut them into strips, and organize and group the strips to form a variety of summaries.
- **Read/Listen**: Read/listen to information and write a summary of the information on a Post-it note. (The summary can't be longer/bigger than a Post-it.)
- **Key Words**: Give students key words from the lesson/text. Prompt students to use each word to write a micro-summary/sentence about the content with that word.
- **Write a 2014 Tweet**: Students read/listen to information and use 140 characters to write their tweet.
- **Word Limit Summary**: Students are given a word limit to write a summary.

Micro-Summarizing Experiences:
- Scissors
- Post-its
- Notecards
- Pair work
- Color coding
- Icon anchoring
- Visual structures
- Whole class work
- Video lessons/information
- Reading/text

OUR PENCIL WAS WRITE... Sitting side by side with my students and their strips of notes cut up in front of them, we started to build a new skill. This time we added an element of the process. "Look at your strips of notes," I said. "Are the strips of information on-topic? Is the information new, is the information interesting, does the information make you feel something?" As students read their strips out loud with me or to themselves they sorted their strips, keeping some and throwing away others. Next, I picked up one of their strips, read it, and thought out loud as I modeled my micro-summarizing of their notes, changing them into a few words, crossing out the words on the strip, and writing in the new micro-summarized phrase. I picked up another strip of notes, reading it out loud, sharing my thinking out loud, crossing out the words on the strip and writing the new micro-summarized phrase on the next strip. With the next and the next strip selected, students began to speak up, share their thinking, share their ideas for micro-summarizing. Suddenly, new micro-summarizing skills began to emerge. Skills that could be practiced and mastered. With their own butcher paper, a pencil, and their strips of micro-summarized notes in front of them, my students began to build their own sketchnotes all by themselves, pairing ideas and information with doodled images and watching their learning and their connections to it come to life.

As we all stood at the table talking, doodling, having conversations about the facts they had organized, and asking questions, I was reminded again of a lesson sketchnoting had taught me so early on. There is no right or wrong way to go on this journey, no right path, no right speed. There is no right or wrong way to bring something new into my classroom…because with the right structures connected to our students' strengths, with words and experiences and time, with a lense that sees tools, tasks, and strategies for what they can do (not what they are made to do), then my students will always be ready to take their turn at this whole sketchnoting thing. And, like always, they will prove to me that it was never that they couldn't. It was never that I couldn't teach them the perfect way or that they couldn't learn it, that we would never make any mistakes, but they would always remind me that not taking the chance would always mean we never got to try.

One random Dana-and-Carrie Sunday at…yes, Panera. Between sips of coffee, Dana and I caught up on what was happening in our classrooms. We shared stories from our classrooms while we updated our session notes with the "whys" of visualizing, and brainstormed activities and stories we could share. We still could not get past this crippling, stuck feeling educators have about putting pencils to paper and doodling. We knew breaking down the "I can't draw" wall was absolutely essential, the first and most important task we would face every single time we would teach/share about sketchnoting. Over our breakfast sandwiches we threw thoughts and ideas at each other. One after the other chipped away at the "I can't draw" wall, but they were just like everyone else's activities for sketchnoting. We knew there had to be a different and more impactful approach.

Intertwined in all the idea sharing, Dana shared how she was using creatures in her classroom. My heart exploded as I listened to her share. The students had created creatures from their imaginations. Dana went on and on, smiling and telling me all about her shy fourth grader who now could share through their creature, and how her students' thinking was getting deeper too.

"Could we use something like that?" she questioned.

My mind was blown. Like mouth wide open, eyes staring, coffee drooling from my mouth in awe.

These creatures could be used to get educators comfortable with drawing. Drawing the same thing over and over again makes it simpler, not so scary. We brainstormed.

"OMG, learning mascots!" I blurted out.

"Like a cheering mascot," Dana smiled, "and it could talk and think about whatever the lesson or learning is about!"

On that Sunday morning at Panera, learning mascots was born: a single image of a single creature, our inner learner, our best self, an image that educators, new sketchnoters, and learners could draw over and over again. A single image that learners could imagine and that they could use to imagine learning.

The very next day (yep, I don't wait when I know an idea is this powerful) I shared our idea with my students. My students spent forty minutes sharing their likes, combining them with visuals, doodling and doodling over and over again until they found their learning mascot. It was incredible. I was left in awe of the visual representations of their inner selves that came out of this simple activity. I was giddy for what these new visuals were going to bring to their learning. I knew this was something special…something very, very special.

Remember me? he nudged.

Hi there. He tapped my shoulder.

Suddenly I was reminded of a day that August when I was unpacking boxes to move into my new classroom. I had seen Snapchat artists adding super fun doodles to their images. I was in awe of their playfulness and use

 of doodles in real life. I wanted to do that too. As I looked at the boxes I had left to unpack, I suddenly had an idea. What if my classroom had a pet? It would need to be something fast and easy to draw…what about a hamster. I picked up my phone, used the drawing option in Snapchat, and drew my very first doodle of a hamster named Stanley. In that same instance, I realized, holy wow, that wasn't even a little simple; it wasn't even easy. How in the world do they create those? More importantly, how would I have time to doodle a hamster over something I took a picture of going on in my classroom to share out while I was trying to teach…what was I thinking!

This little guy decided he didn't want to let me forget him that easily. As my students smiled and connected with their learning mascots, he whispered to me, giggled, and talked to me. He wasn't just a class hamster doodle, a silly, fleeting idea. He was my alter ego…he was everything I was, wanted to be, dreamed I was!

My students had found their learning mascots, and so had I. The Sundays that followed were bookends of giddy, giggly, happy texts about what Dana and I were seeing in our classrooms. The impact the learning mascots were having—on our students' growth, their learning, the connections to themselves, the moments that were showing their incredible potential, and learning being visualized—was too powerful. It left us exploding with happiness too powerful to deny—this power we had found in this simple, single doodle.

We started to wonder. This idea of visualizing an inner learner, it couldn't possibly be something two educators from Illinois, sitting at a Panera, sipping coffee, were the first ever to think up. There had to be science that backed it up.

We weren't that good. Dana and I knew it was time to dive in and do some research. What we found supported everything we were seeing in our classrooms—learning mascots were powered by so much more than just some kids' imaginations and two teachers' gut feeling that this was awesome stuff. And oh boy, were we right about the research backing these single doodles.

First, there is metacognition, or "thinking about our thinking." Learning mascots cause us to think actively, strategically strengthening the connections we make to learning. What Dana and I saw in our classrooms was that learning mascots were allowing our learners to take in information, assess, reflect, and wonder, all through a self-created doodle that

was in their brains, that voiced their thinking. It challenged them to slow down and think about how and what they were thinking, and it forced them to connect it to their learning. It pushed them to self-reflect, self-assess, iterate, change, grow, and move forward.

If that wasn't powerful enough (and

heck yeah, we knew we were on to something), there was also dual coding. We knew dual coding assumed that the two sides of our brain were separate but connected. Basically, we have two halves of our brains, and one thinks in words and the other thinks in pictures. When they work together, the connections, and our learning, is stronger and more solidified. What we saw with learning mascots was it allowed our students to take in information visually or audibly, visualize a single, familiar image, pair it with their learning, and then solidify the learning by doodling the learning mascot with their words.

Next we learned of learning mascots' rich connection to externalization. For me this was one of the most deeply moving effects of learning mascots. "Externalization" means to change from a mental image into a "real" object. It is when we imagine an image so that we can create an explanation for our inner problem. When therapists use externalization strategies, they empower children to see that the problem is separate from themselves, that there is nothing bad about them or wrong with them; it is the problem that needs to be faced because "when the problem is the problem,  you can activate to improve your situation without this meaning that you are somehow bad...without it meaning you have to change the person you think you are."[1]

We also realized that learning mascots were a consistent, simple icon: a single, quick, simple-to-draw, well-practiced doodle that was a consistent visual for students' learning. Learning mascots allowed learners

---

[1] Schreiner, Michael. "Externalizing Conversations." Evolution Counseling. January 20, 2015. https://evolutioncounseling.com/externalizing-conversations/.

and creators to have one single image they could draw quickly and simply over and over again to show learning, connections, reflections, understanding...you name it! It also empowered inexperienced or hesitant doodlers to put their pencils to paper and start connecting their learning and experiences to doodles. Double bonus!

Then I was reminded of a powerful tool from my past, back in the day when I was a high school athlete: visualization. "Visualization is a cognitive tool accessing imagination to realize all aspects of an ob-

ject, action or outcome. This may include recreating a mental sensory experience of sound, sight, smell, taste, and touch."[2] Athletes, speakers, or people fighting an illness use it to see in their mind the experience they want to be the outcome. It is also a tool therapists use to help patients see the outcome they want, or as a relaxation strategy (imagine a Hawaiian beach with crystal blue water, sandy beach, and sun on your face, and try not to go to your happy place). Visualization paired with a concrete visual (learning mascot) is a super powerful combination of awesome stuff happening. A learning mascot can be visualized, doodled, doing powerful things that we want to see ourselves doing.

Now it is time for you to say hello to your own learning mascot…

---

2 "Visualize It." Psychology Today. https://www.psychologytoday.com/us/blog/the-psychology-dress/201111/visualize-it.

The learning mascots' impact on us didn't stop at the table at Panera. It was inspiring to go beyond the research, experience these creatures in action in our classrooms, and see the power it gave our students.

It wasn't long before these little creatures became so much more than a doodle on a page with a talk bubble.

A single drawing, a doodle in the margin connected to new thinking, and an old process suddenly contains infinite potential, infinite possibilities to impact so much. With each line, curve, thought bubble, swirl, a single drawing and talk bubble reminds us of our infinite potential to take on whatever life and learning brings us, and give back to it infinite amounts of our awesome! There was so much Dana and I wanted to share and teach others about this tool we were so very passionate about: learning mascots.

① what is its story?

② what does it need to grow?

③ what are 5 facts about your learning mascot?

④ what legacy does it leave?

* what does it say when things get hard?

* what does its heart look like?

[Learning Mascot pic]

height:
age:
lives:

Now that we had tackled the "I can't draw" mindset, we knew there was another mindset that needed help. It was moving past the fear, the freezing from thinking that sketchnoting has to be this enormous work. This thinking that it was an all-or-nothing task also had to be broken and destroyed. Hour after hour we would brainstorm over coffee at Panera, until one Sunday we took our experiences, learning, and research and realized it wasn't a *complete* sketchnote that made it so powerful; the incredible power was in its *parts*.

We knew sketchnoting elements and visual thinking didn't have to be an all-or-nothing task. It didn't have to be an only-this-way activity. We knew that there was so much more power packed into sketchnoting that was just waiting to be unleashed on others. It was time others understand it too. It was time that sketchnoting, visual thinking, and doodling to learn (whatever you called it) was exactly what you needed it to be for you. It was time we looked beyond the overpowering, daunting beauty that others produced, and looked at what each element of sketchnoting (told you I would come back to it) would do for students. It was time that there were no more limits…there are no rules! But for all of this to work, we also knew that…

…two things needed to happen for this kind of crazy to work.

One, in order to connect others to the power of sketchnoting, visual thinking, and doodling to learn, we had to empower others to get over themselves, pick up a pencil and doodle. Well, learning mascots totally crushed that, but we would need to add a few more activities. This single act—drawing with students, drawing by yourself, drawing with friends, drawing with your children—will have the greatest impact on others picking up a pencil and drawing. Also, let's be honest, you can never have enough doodles in your life. Doodles awaken our brains, bring learning and information to life, enhance information's meaning, solidify its connection in our brains, and connect our learning, our ideas, and our experiences.

Two, getting educators to connect with and see the value in visualizing was the easy part. Reading and ELA instructors, special educators, speech and language pathologists…um…adults, readers, children, human beings have used visualization techniques for decades. We just needed to remind them of their training, their learning, their experiences, and the power of this thinking connected with doodling.

With the "I can't draw" wall crushed, our peeps (yep, that's you too) connected with their learning mascots. It was time to take down this beast that is the all-encompassing, beautifully colored, perfectly drawn, masterfully created sketchnote. Go ahead and pick up your phone. Do a Google search for "sketchnotes." I'll wait.

Back? A smidge soul crushing, huh? Now, what if I told you that a sketchnote's power isn't in those whole pictures. The power is in the parts.

See, as Dana and I sat there idea-sharing and brainstorming, something suddenly occurred to us. It was what we both saw in our classrooms each day. The power of visual thinking and doodling to learn was never in the sketchnote. The incredible power was in its parts.

Carrie Baughcum

Topic

Definition: The main thing the sketchnote is about.

Purpose: To focus thinking and identify relationships between information and images.

Power: Topic keeps us on task and gives us focus. "Is that fact about this topic? Yes, add it. No, let it go." Topic directs our understanding of supporting ideas/details. It anchors all information back to a single thing. It is the box our brain fills with all the facts we are learning, adding to, or amplifying.

How can we use topic's power and thinking differently to enhance our visual thinking and doodling to learn?

Topics do not just come in words. Topics can be a single picture that anchors the information learned about it or observed within it.

Topics do not have to come in a single word. Quotes and phrases can be powerful igniters for visualizing learning and doodling the detailed, colorful, and powerful movie in our head inspired by the words.

TOPIC PRACTICE
ideas for adding the power of topic to visual thinking and doodling to learn

Carrie Baughcum

Typography

Definition: How we write the words. It is bold versus regular letter writing, cursive versus block lettering, all-caps versus lowercase writing.

Purpose: Typography can show the importance of information, organize words/phrases, emphasize major ideas, and show the mood.

Power: Think of fonts as words on visual steroids with superpowers. They can make our brains pay special attention to information, visually organize words, anchor similar information, and connect our feelings to information.

How can we use typography's power and thinking differently to enhance our visual thinking and doodling to learn?

Text captures the meaning of words, quotes, and key points. It enables us to avoid trying to summarize everything and instead empowers us to give it visual emphasis.

Fonts can also combine with "the movie in our head" to create powerful single-word images that express connections, anchor information, and visualize our learning.

TOPIC PRACTICE
ideas for adding the power of typography to visual thinking and doodling to learn

Icons

Definition: Simple objects and images drawn to show what we are imagining.

Purpose: To activate the visual part of our brains and connect the information we are taking in with a visual.

Power: To bring information to life, enhance our understanding, organize our thoughts, improve expressive language, give others a peek into our thinking, connect current knowledge with new learning, and improve critical thinking. Icons link information, language, and thought to an image.

Now, we have already talked, um, a TON about icons! They hold ridiculous power. When we read or hear information, we form a picture or play a movie in our heads. We take the image we are imagining and connect

it to an icon and/or words. This improves our comprehension. Then we put pencil to paper and doodle the information we learned, paired with the image we imagined. Icons improve our retention, recall, focus, and listening skills. Sketchnoting calms us and makes us happy: this is its superpower, its mojo, its holy wow, its huge, big, humongous boom pow. (For greater detail, remember we talked about this in Part 3: Visualizing, and Part 1: Discover.)

This before all else, before all other elements, is what I layer over and add to what I am already doing in my classroom. This is the skill I make sure each learner can do before we go any further. Just this single element, this single process, this single intentional act will have a "never look back" and "oh my word" impact on learning. It is a skill that can be accessed and practiced with any subject, by any age group, and for any reason.

How can we use icon's power and thinking differently to enhance our visual thinking and doodling to learn?

Reading or hearing information, visualizing it, and doodling what we visualize can happen anywhere, with any subject, with all learning.

While the thought of how many potential icons we might have to "know how to draw" is a daunting thought to some, icons can also have their very own icon thesaurus. A thesaurus is a book that lists words in groups of synonyms and related con-

cepts. In a predefined icon thesaurus, preselected icons represent specific synonyms or related words.

Each single visual, each single doodle, strengthens our learning and our connections to the information and improves so many parts of our learning.

Ideas for adding the "there are no rules" power of icons to your visual thinking and doodling to learn:

TOPIC PRACTICE
ideas for adding the power of icons to visual thinking and doodling to learn

Dividers, Arrows, and Connectors

Definition: Arrows (fat, short, circular, etc.), dashed lines, dotted lines, just lines (straight, curvy, any), swirls, zigzags, etc.

Purpose: They show relationships among ideas and/or concepts. They connect ideas, pieces of stories, or information. They help show direction and visual sequence.

Power: They are organizers and visual directors. They provide structure, anchor information, and visually depict relationships. They organize information and visuals with a visual.

How can we use the power of dividers, arrows, and connectors and thinking differently to enhance our visual thinking and doodling to learn?

Ideas for adding the power of dividers, arrows and connectors to your visual thinking and doodling to learn:

TOPIC PRACTICE
ideas for adding the power of dividers, arrows and connectors to visual thinking and doodling to learn

Containers

Definition: Squares, circles, rectangles, thought bubbles, clouds, talk bubbles, comic bam, and banners that hold information or ideas.

Purpose: To hold words, information, and ideas. To organize information visually. To visually connect like information. To add emphasis, meaning, or purpose to information in a sketchnote.

Power: They can sort information, show hierarchy, anchor information, provide structure, or be used to categorize information.

How can we use the power of containers and thinking differently to enhance our visual thinking and doodling to learn?

Containers can sort information, provide structure, or be used to categorize information. Who said the organizer could only be a basic shape? What if the container was the topic, a visual topic that anchored all information in it to that visual? How much do you know about apples?

Containers also have the power to anchor information. Using one common container for information repeatedly can not only anchor information, trigger processes, and prompt action, it can also organize and synthesize information. Add some color coding to containers with similar information and boom-pow: all kinds of bonus anchoring.

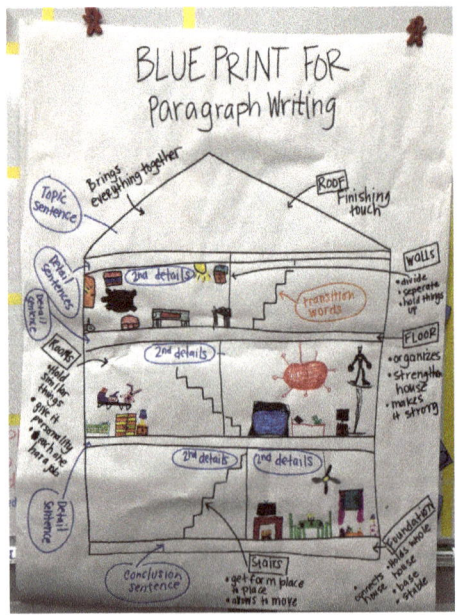

Ideas for adding the "there are no rules" power of containers to your visual thinking and doodling to learn:

```
┌─TOPIC PRACTICE ──────────────────────┐
│  ideas for adding the power of containers to
│  visual thinking and doodling to learn
│
│
│
│
│
│
│
│
│
└──────────────────────────────────────┘
```

Structure

Definition: How we lay out, organize, and plan our sketchnote.

Purpose: Sketchnotes come in many shapes and infinite styles and can be affected by anything from the topic to the sketchnoter's doodle style, learning strengths/weaknesses, level of experience with visual thinking and sketchnoting, visualization skill, micro-summarizing skill, and/or feelings about the information and learning.

Power: To follow the flow of the sketchnoter's mind through the connections they are inspired to make, to wherever the feelings or overall mood takes them.

My Pencil Made Me Do It

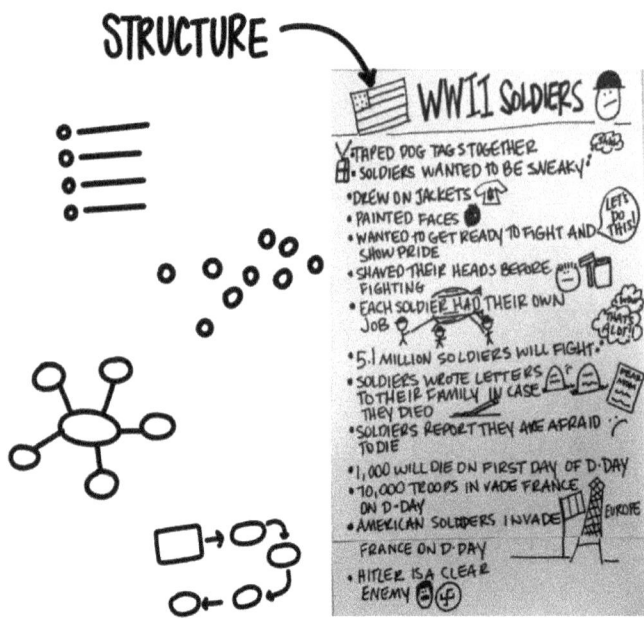

How can we use structure's power and thinking differently to enhance our visual thinking and doodling to learn?

Sketchnotes' structure are as individual as people. Visually, sketchnotes can be organized in multiple ways, each with its own strength.

Vertical sketchnotes are up and down, just like traditional notes. Each fact is concise, structured, and on-topic. Each fact is micro-summarized to solidify learning and then connected with a consistent visual.

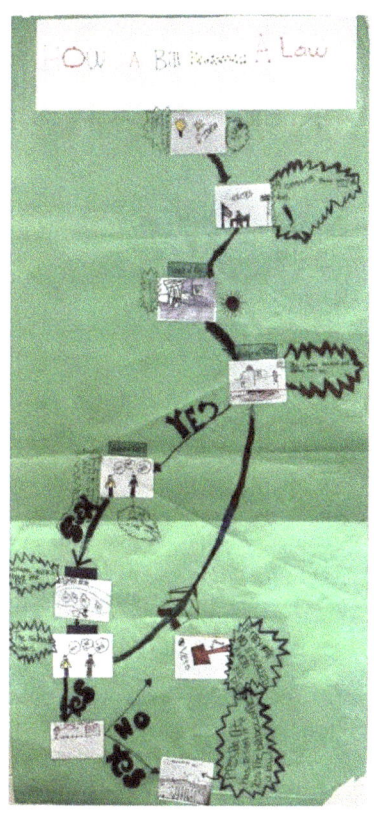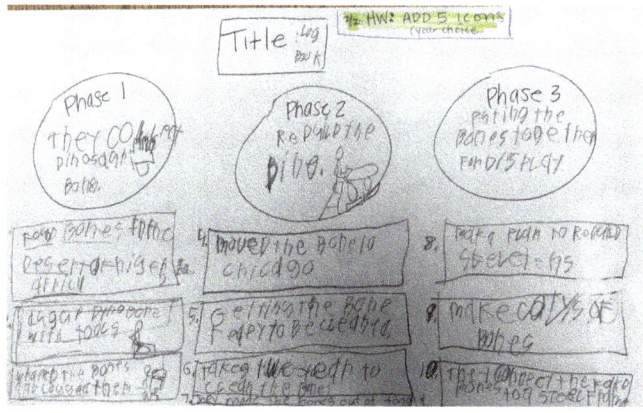

Information we record in a sketchnote can follow a variety of different planning styles. Each of us takes in and organizes information differently. The emphasis should be on connecting with what way works for us best, being comfortable with it ebbing, what we are sketchnoting, and allowing it to grow as we grow, and most of all, knowing and believing that there is no right way, no wrong way, and no only one way to structure a sketchnote. Each structure holds strength and power for different thinkers and each learner.

- Linear (good for processes/time progression and can be horizontal or vertical)
- Pathway (time progression/goals)
- Columns (different speakers/topics/ideas)
- Read Like a Book (top/bottom and left to right)
- Box Planning/Comic Book Style
- Central Idea or Radial (concept mapping)
- Hot Mess Express

Ideas for adding the "there are no rules" power of structure to your visual thinking and doodling to learn:

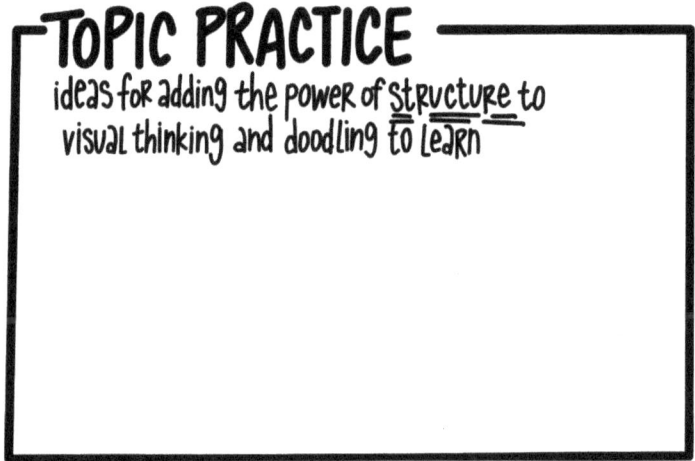

Carrie Baughcum

Shading/Coloring

Definition: Color, dimension, and/or shading added to your sketchnote.

Purpose: To show importance, highlight organization, and categorize information and images.

Power: To visually organize information and anchor information in the brain, improving retention and recall. It breaks up information for the eyes and can make important information stand out.

How can we use shading/coloring's power and thinking differently to enhance our visual thinking and doodling to learn?

How you color, shade, and add emphasis is up to you! Your sketchnote doesn't need to be a coloring book. Use one color or use many… yep, there are no rules. Add color before you start to pre-organize your sketchnote, add it as you go, or save coloring until the end. Use color to show importance, organize information, share favorite ideas, anchor information, and/or categorize facts.

My Pencil Made Me Do It

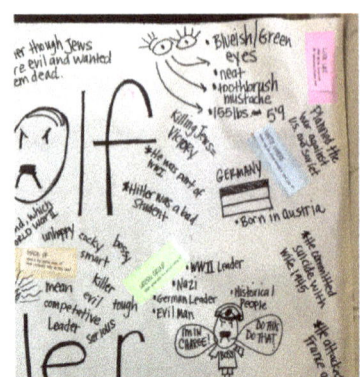

Create a Class Color Key

Ex. Use the same color each time on all sketchnotes: Green is for names, blue is for actions, pink is for questions, and yellow is for takeaways.

Ideas for adding the "there are no rules" power of shading and color to your visual thinking and doodling to learn:

Carrie Baughcum

TOPIC PRACTICE
ideas for adding the power of <u>shading and color</u> to visual thinking and doodling to <u>learn</u>

Part 6: REPEAT

Since the first time "What movie is playing in your head?" was said in my classroom, sketchnote elements have been ever present there. Every lesson that visual thinking and doodling to learn have taught me continues to be present every day, while its power and energy infuses, invades, and enriches my life in ways I couldn't possibly imagine. Whether it is icons in the margins, using a class-created color key to organize notes or sketchnotes in the shape of houses, we connect everything to visuals. From visualizing a math problem, to talking about what a story made us imagine, to doodling what a fact means in social studies or color-coding parts of a paragraph, visuals are everywhere. This process, this skill, this ability that I could never have imagined my

students learning, let alone possessing, is one of the greatest gifts I give as a teacher.

Since the first learning mascot was drawn, every year we take time to be reminded of our inner doodler, connect with our inner us, unlock hidden details of our personalities, shine a light on the incredible parts of us that we often forget, remind ourselves that we can (and maybe we even like…er, remember loving to) draw. In one simple activity, everyone in my classroom is given permission to create, to think, to be themselves, to draw, and to imagine their own way. As my students grow (I get to work with my students for three years), so do their learning mascots. One year their

learning mascot's legacy may be to make others laugh; the next they want to be that student who can be there for others, then the one who can help others on homework during resource class. One year they may see themselves as a basketball, unable to see themselves as more than an object connected to what they love. The next year their learning mascot is a cartoon-figure basketball player, now not only a reflection of their love, but also their real selves. Just like I get to watch my students grow, change, and see more in themselves through their learning mascots, the learning mascots grow, too. Something that can start as a seemingly simple, single doodle, today represents the inner us, leaves a legacy, whispers positive affirmations to us when things are hard, shares our thinking, reveals our thoughts about life, and enhances our learning.

Every year since that first rogue moment, I am reminded of the power of seeing past a disability, cognitive level, perceived skill ability, or restraints. The change that can come from ignoring the "it has to be this way" and "it has always been done like this." The difference that can be made in deciding to see what they are capable of, what their individual strengths bring, and connecting them with learning tools that show them anything is possible when we look past the rules and look toward the possibilities. This mindset, paired with experiences and new learning, continues to infuse and grow in my classroom every single day. It is a journey that I am consistently blown away by.

A single Instagram reply to a friend who reached out with a crazy idea sparked something big: *What if on January 11, World Sketchnote Day, two educators with one crazy idea asked other educators and creators if they wanted to play Pass the Sketchnote, where teams of passionate doodlers pass a sketchnote around the world and back.* In our second year, 200 strangers came together in 39 teams in 160 countries to join us in celebrating everything that is

awesome about doodles, drawing, people, creating, and joining together to bring out incredible things in each other.

Today, my children and I can still be seen sitting together at a table, creating and drawing together. The love language that once was only spoken by them is a language we now speak together and often. It is a language that has become a part of our everyday lives, a language that has matured into creative fearlessness, confidence, and a deep love for creating and drawing together. It is a love that has sparked ideas and inspired us to create and dream big, and it has inspired moments...

Moments like when my youngest decided that she loved drawing with us so much that we should draw together on the same piece of paper, on the same topic, record it, and then share that video (like on YouTube... gulp) out for the world to see. Infused with smiles, laughs, sharing stories, and creating memories, just one time was not enough. Sitting on our living room floor surrounded by markers, the computer open to the thesaurus tab, and papers spread in front of us, she wrote words over and over in different combinations.

"Idea flood," she smiled and laughed.

"I love it," I answered.

In that single moment, fueled by shared smiles, memories, the warmth of drawing, and a love of creating together, the Idea Flood Sketchnote monthly challenge was born. Each month my children and I would create a video sharing out a single topic, and ask others from all over the world (OK, whoever out

there happened to be listening) to turn on their thinkers, activate their doodle makers, and flood their paper with words and images about the topic. They would share their #IdeaFlood with us. We would gather them all up and share them in a wrap-up video at the end of the month.

Suddenly my sketchnoting journey was right back where it had started. I was right back with my children and our table.

As we look at our journeys, we cannot predict where they will take us. We can, instead, begin to see each experience with our students differently. We can begin to see the unlimited potential and infinite possibilities just waiting to connect with us, waiting to be discovered, and start to see an opportunity not revealed by a world full of shoulda, only this way, must, only that way, or have to; a moment opened by those of

us who can look at others, look at creating, at learning, look within themselves and see what is out there. Who can see what the world holds, those things just waiting for us to seize them and use them to bring out the very best in those we teach, what we create, how we learn, how we teach, and the incredibly amazing parts in each of us. And all it took was a pencil, paper, a table, and a few awesome people!

About the Author

Carrie Baughcum is a mother, wife, mismatch sock wearer, a self-described inspiration junkie, learning enthusiast, and most of all a passionate believer that all children can learn, we just need to find out how. As a special education teacher of 20+ years, she integrates technology, creative thinking, a fearless attitude, the power of gamification and endless doodles into her classroom. She strives every day to enhance her students' learning while empowering them to achieve things they never knew they could do or be a part of. She is also the mother to two children, 12 and 13 years old. At home she encourages her children to explore, learn, and try anything their imaginations can think up. Together they create and get involved in activities and experiences with exploration, creativity, problem-solving and making.

Carrie shares her experiences from her classroom, her adventures, reflections on her time with her husband, children, and students by speaking and connecting with others at conferences and sharing on youtube.com/carriebaughcum and at carriebaughcum.com.

www.ingramcontent.com/pod-product-compliance
Lightning Source LLC
Chambersburg PA
CBHW040304170426
43194CB00021B/2891